REINVENT YOUR CAREER

REINVENT
YOUR
CAREER

Beat Age Discrimination
to Land Your Dream Job

By
DIANE HUTH, MA, MBA

Published by

ISLA
Publishing Group

San Antonio, TX

REINVENT YOUR CAREER
Beat Age Discrimination to Land Your Dream Job
By
Diane Huth, MA, MBA

PUBLISHER'S NOTE:

This publication is designed to provide accurate information at the time of publication. It is published with the understanding that the author and publisher are not engaged in rendering legal, accounting or other professional services. If you require legal or financial advice or expert assistance, you should seek the services of a competent professional.

Any brand names or logos are used in an editorial fashion, and the author and publisher claim no relationship with or ownership of companies other than specifically noted herein. Any recommendations for action, vendors or service providers are the sole opinion of the author. Names and contact information for job search tools, scripts or other document examples may be based on real people, but their names and contact information have been changed to protect their privacy.

TABLE OF CONTENTS

INTRODUCTION. 1

SECTION 1 THE BABY BOOMER EMPLOYMENT CRISIS. 7

   1. The Unemployment Crisis That No One Is Talking About . . . 9

   2. Does Age Discrimination Really Exist In America Today?. . . 11

   3. But Isn't Age Discrimination Against The Law? 15

   4. So Why DO Companies Prefer Millennials Today? 18

   5. Ten Reasons They Should Hire YOU Instead of a Millennial . . 26

SECTION 2 HOW TO KEEP OR LAND A JOB IN CORPORATE AMERICA 37

   6. TECH UP!. 39

   7. Embrace Life-Long Learning to Up Your Skills 44

   8. Look as Young As You Can Without Looking Silly 50

   9. Adopt Younger Actions, Habits, Tools and Props 75

   10. Develop a More Youthful Communication Style 81

SECTION 3 - BRAND YOURSELF TO SHIFT-PROOF YOUR CAREER 87

   11. Double Down on Networking 89

   12. Start Your Own Consulting Company 97

   13. Master Your Social Media Presence. 104

   14. Build a Powerful Résumé 114

   15. Gather All Your Job Search Tools and Credentials 129

SECTION 4 - SO WHAT DO YOU REALLY WANT TO DO? 137

16. Revise Your Earnings Expectations 139

17. The Concept of "Retirement" Has Changed 143

18. What Are Your Personal Passions? 145

19. Figure Out Your Lifestyle Changes As You Age. 149

20. If You Win the Lottery Today... 152

SECTION 5 - MAKE FINANCIAL AND LIFESTYLE CHOICES NOW 159

21. Become Frugal at Fifty 161

22. Home Sweet Home...Or Is It? 164

23. Lower Expenses to Your Retirement Level Now 173

24. Now's The Time To Reinvent Your Career 175

TAKE THE NEXT STEP TO FIND MEANINGFUL EMPLOYMENT 177

MEET THE AUTHOR 179

THANKS TO VERY SPECIAL PEOPLE 181

IMAGE LICENSES 182

RESOURCE GUIDE 183

INDEX 187

MORE BOOKS IN THE BRAND YOU! SERIES OF CAREER GUIDES 192

BEFORE YOU GO 192

THE BABY BOOMER JOB CRISIS AND HOW TO BEAT IT

Corporate America has a dirty little secret — companies are tossing out their baby boomer employees like yesterday's newspaper. We are being replaced by younger (and cheaper) millennials — relatively new college grads who have a fraction of our experience, wisdom, people skills, and industry and company history.

We Have Become the Unemployable Generation

Corporations are simply not hiring workers in their 50s, 60s, much less 70s. But with Social Security eligibility age being pushed to 67 and soon to 70, and the average American lifespan extending into the 80s, workers will want and need to work well into their 60s and 70s. Medical insurance premiums for anyone 55 or older often cost more than $1,000 a month, especially if you have a pre-existing condition of any kind. That forces workers to find a job if only to keep their company medical benefits until they qualify for Medicare at 65. Otherwise they risk being devastated by exorbitant premiums in addition to huge medical deductibles for needed care.

Over the years, we've lost the traditional retirement safety net we were promised when we started our careers 30 or 40 years ago. There's no gold watch at the end of three decades of work like previous generations received. In the 1970s, Corporate America realized that pension liabilities were huge and growing exponentially, due to the demographic trends of a much longer life span. So with government support, corporations shifted the retirement liability from their own pension funds to the shoulders of employees, in the form of voluntary IRA savings accounts. Those funds are now subject to the whims of the market, as many mature workers learned, when a quarter of Americans 50 years and older lost all their savings during the 2007-2009 recession.

So how will we handle the disparity of being unemployable 10 or 20 years before we are ready to "retire"? The numbers don't work, and we are caught in the crosshairs of a major demographic cataclysm that is imperiling the survivability of a whole generation of Americans.

But It Doesn't Have to Be That Way

The good news is that the new historic low unemployment levels have created a great demand for skilled employees — like YOU!

When I woke up this morning, the economic news heralded the lowest unemployment levels in 45 years and a shortage of skilled workers nationwide. So Corporate America needs you…but how do you get in the door to persuade them that you are the right candidate with the skills and experience they need?

Front line recruiters are often young lower-level managers, who may not value your experience and wisdom like the CEO or a senior-level hiring manager would. Therefore, you may never get a chance to meet them on an interview if you pursue traditional career search protocol. It's possible to get a job in Corporate America, but it may not be easy. It takes an understanding of the situation and taking steps to lessen the impact your age has on your career opportunities. It often requires changing your mindset to help you overcome the subconscious prejudice that recruiters feel when interviewing someone older, with white hair, and often with more experience than the hiring manager. That's why I wrote this book: to help guide you through the labyrinthine process of revamping your career skill set, your appearance, your communication style, and much more, to help you get a good job in your 50s, 60, even 70s.

What Compelled Me to Write This Book

My name is Diane Huth, and I've worked in marketing and branding in Corporate America for many leading global brands for 40 years. I recently started teaching marketing at two different universities and was stunned to learn that my bright talented students didn't have a clue about how to find a job when they graduated. I wrote my first book, *BRAND YOU! To Land Your Dream Job*, to teach them how to use the marketing skills I teach in class to market the most important product — themselves.

But then something amazing happened. I was quietly, shyly, timidly contacted by many of my friends and peers, competent talented professionals I knew, had worked with, trusted and held in high regard. They were asking for my help. They were desperate, depressed, wounded and confused. They were subsisting on food stamps and unemployment benefits, doing manual labor on a farm for a place to live, evicted from their homes and living in cars, ashamed that their wives were supporting them, often bewildered at the sudden loss of employability after decades of being a corporate rock star. I had an Uber driver pull over on the side of the road and burst into tears as she told me how she couldn't get a job after 12 years as a Project Manager in the IT department of a Fortune 100 company. I was stunned and saddened to talk with an experienced process engineer formerly with a blue chip high tech firm who was practically shaking in rage and frustration when he told me of his two-year battle to land even a single interview.

I discovered that there is a legion of outstanding professionals who have been discarded by Corporate America for one reason alone — their age. These educated, experienced, wise professionals in their 50s and 60s were being replaced by millennials, who companies seek out to help them address today's market of younger consumers. Then these mature professionals at the height of their careers were tossed aside and unable to find work.

In fact, I realized that I was vulnerable to the exact same unfair discrimination. After all, I'd just turned 67 — that's past traditional retirement age. No one is going to hire a 67 year old marketing head — that's a job for the 34 year-old whiz kids today, like I was way back then. And I certainly wasn't ready to "retire" and lose my income and my status as a valuable contributing professional. But when you can't find a job in your career field, when you can't be gainfully employed doing what you know and love, what can you do?

To help my friends and former colleagues, I started studying and researching to understand the dynamics of this job displacement phenomenon. I talked extensively with angry, frustrated and traumatized baby boomers hurting from the loss of income to support their families, and the loss of their professional and often personal identities. I talked with on-the-move millennials who were swelling the ranks of Corporate America in the jobs last held by my peers, who couldn't see themselves hiring older workers. I talked with CEOs to find out what the issues were from their point of view. I also talked with older workers who had moved on into new and creative roles not open to them before.

I slowly but surely started to understand the dynamics of this job shift, and realized that it didn't need to be this way.

I discovered the reasons Corporate America needs us and how we have to communicate the unique skills and talents that set us apart favorably from the current younger generation.

I learned that the same personal branding tools, which I taught younger college grads, apply to us baby boomers as well — some of which give us a strong competitive advantage if we know how to leverage them.

I discovered five key ways older workers must adapt to fit into today's new younger workplace to keep or get highly-paid corporate positions. I share those tips and techniques in detail in this book.

Just as importantly, I realized that we may have a better and different calling — to reinvent ourselves and our careers by exploiting our unique talents in new ways, rather than trying to compete with younger workers for the same jobs we held decades ago.

We can and should reinvent ourselves and our careers to find meaningful work using our many decades of skills that we are uniquely qualified to tap into. And in the process, we can redefine what "retirement", "career" and "work" can and should be to provide long term satisfaction.

I'm driven to share these insights and discoveries with fellow professionals in their 50s and 60s and even 70s, to help us re-imagine and create a vision of the future as encompassing meaningful, well-compensated, important work that we can enjoy and contribute to for as long as we wish to remain productive and active.

Our World Has Shifted — And So Must We

The nature of our work throughout our lives has changed as we have aged, with our first 20-plus years as full-time students. We didn't earn money and we often paid dearly for our formal educations. We embarked on our careers with great enthusiasm, learning and gaining vast experiences. Throughout our careers, we have had many transformations. The average American changes careers (not jobs) every 8 to 10 years, with 3 to 5 different careers in a lifetime.

Think of this period of life as another phase or transformation in our journey of lifelong learning and contributing to society while supporting ourselves and our families.

In fact, people tend to reinvent themselves on average every seven to ten years. That's why universities traditionally provide their professors with a sabbatical every seven years to do something different — write, travel, study, research, whatever. That's not a new concept; sabbaticals hark back to biblical times, and refer to the Sabbath, which is the seventh day of the week. That's also why people frequently divorce at the 7, 15 or 20-year mark, as the personality and lifestyle changes become too much to sustain for many couples, both of whom are undergoing dramatic changes at the same time.

What we do in the future doesn't need to be the same as we have been doing for the past 20 or 30 or 40 years. We can change, and so can our careers. That can mean a change in the type of work we do, in the level of challenge, in the time dedicated to our jobs, where we work geographically, whether we work in an office or from home or even on the road. It can embrace less traditional work structures, including part time work, contract work, time shifting and job sharing, and occasional or gig employment.

Futurists project that in the next ten years, almost half of all professional jobs will be done as contract labor, another big shift from the traditional full-time jobs we've enjoyed in the past. Millions of us will work as independent contractors or contingent workers rather than full time salaried employees. We may also choose to work as sole proprietors, or form corporations or LLCs as part of owning and running our own business. We may want to embrace the "gig economy", a work and lifestyle shift of dramatic proportions.

Plus, we will probably need to make changes in the way we look at our homes and lifestyles, particularly if we can't count on a steady flow of income for decades on end.

It's all a life in transformation, motivated by and reflected in our career shifts. It goes deep into the fiber of our beings.

Why You Should Read This Book

In this book, we will walk step-by-step through the changes in the workplace, and how you can adapt to these transformations to succeed in meeting your career goals:

- Learn why employers have been hiring younger workers, and how you can find your place in today's shifting employment market.
- Discover your unique benefits to an employer, and how to position your skills, experience, maturity and wisdom to make you the best candidate for a key position.

- Explore how to erase 10 to 15 years off your personal presence to fit in better with a younger workforce, so you can keep your seniority on the team without looking like you're the grandparent of a new colleague.
- Learn to erase the barriers of perceived age in how you act and interact, so you will better fit into a younger workforce.
- Embrace today's technology to "Tech Up" to start to bridge the technology gap inherent in today's workplace.
- Master a key asset which we mature workers enjoy — our network, created through decades of contacts and colleagues, which should be a key benefit in your career going forward.

How We Baby Boomers Identify Ourselves

One of our biggest challenges as we look at the changing workplace is how we look at ourselves. Our generation was raised to identify ourselves by our jobs or careers — "I'm a Banker", or "I'm a Marketer," or a Nurse, or an Engineer, or a Salesman.

Today, those roles are shifting, and we may find ourselves working in several different careers or fields simultaneously. When people ask me what I do, today I reply, *"I'm the poster child for multiple streams of income. I'm the VP of Marketing for Biovideo, I am a Marketing Professor at two universities, I'm an Innovation Consultant for Prodigy Works, and I'm an Author and Public Speaker and Career Coach."* That is symptomatic of how our careers will change in the future as we reinvent ourselves, and we must feel comfortable with that change.

Younger workers describe themselves more by their personal attributes, hobbies and lifestyles, and less by their profession. My son, age 29, describes himself as a *"husband, son, homeowner, cook, rugby player, avid reader, doggy daddy, fitness lover, and that he makes a living working in marketing and project management for a high-tech company."*

These are very different perspectives of how we see ourselves. Neither is right nor wrong, just different perspectives indicative of different generations.

Throughout the book I will offer you downloadable worksheets, bonus content, lists of referrals and resources, and much more. You can access them from my webpage *www.BrandYouGuide.com*.

Also, please sign up for my weekly newsletter and update with valuable information at *FindMyDreamJobNow.com*.

THE BABY BOOMER EMPLOYMENT CRISIS

Economists and politicians talk about the Social Security crisis, with money running out because of the demographics of baby boomers. Politicians wrangle about funding Social Security and Medicare and threaten that checks won't go out if the budget isn't passed. Conservatives argue that Social Security would have been just fine, thank you very much, if Lyndon B. Johnson hadn't stolen the reserve funds in 1968 to pay for government deficits. Liberals talk about Medicare and Medicaid as if the programs were one and the same. They argue about who should pay their "fair share," and accuse the other party of trying to take Medicare away from seniors and "killing grandma."

The good news is that Social Security and Medicare are just fine, and we baby boomers will get the money we have earned.

But the real crisis starts long before anyone ever gets to Social Security and Medicare age.

THE UNEMPLOYMENT CRISIS THAT NO ONE IS TALKING ABOUT

One of the most dramatic changes in the workforce is us — the baby boomer generation, more than 76 million men and women alive today who were born between 1946 and 1964.

The US workforce has traditionally been fed by younger workers in their 20s, 30s and 40s, with a mandatory maximum retirement age of 65. Corporate America's workers were primarily men, except for a smattering of low paid jobs held by women.

Women didn't really join Corporate America until the late 1970s and 1980s, during the years of the Women's Lib movement (now called the Feminist movement) led by Gloria Steinem. Prior to that, professional jobs for women consisted almost exclusively of nurses, teachers, airline stewardesses, secretaries and clerical workers. A few decades ago, there were few precedents for professional women employed in interesting, well-paid and rewarding careers. I remember clearly, because I was there and you probably were too.

Life expectancy has skyrocketed from age 47 for a man born in 1900, to 83 if born in 1950 and is still alive today. Women on average live several years longer than men, so the average woman living today can expect to live into her late 80s.

The NRA (National Retirement Age) for Social Security was established in 1935 as being age 65. The average life expectancy of men born in 1900 — age 35 at the time at the time the law was enacted — was just 47. So Social Security was set up to support a small percentage of very old surviving workers for a few scant years of life, when many of their children were no longer alive or able to support them.

All that has changed as we now expect to live well into our late 80s and futurists and vegetarian nutritionists talk about living to age 105 or later.

Traditionally, before the evisceration of pension plans and their replacements with IRAs, retirement was mandatory after 30 years of service, so a worker who started working when he was 20 would retire with a gold watch and full pension benefits at the age of 50. A few decades ago, no one would have imagined an entire generation of healthy workers in their 60s and 70s wanting to work — it was unheard of.

Social Security benefits are calculated taking into consideration the highest-earning 35 years of employment and maximum contribution to receive maximum benefits. The formula is confusing, but we will have to work full time at the highest possible salary right up to the day we retire to make sure we earn enough in Social Security benefits to sustain us as we grow older.

One of the biggest changes our generation has faced is the elimination of pension plans funded by companies, and the subsequent wholesale conversion of retirement responsibility from employers, to individuals through tax deductions and token profit-sharing or by matching contributions to IRAs. Our savings can't span the gap between being forced to retire from the workforce at 50 or 55, required to fund exorbitant medical insurance premiums for five, ten or more years before being eligible for Medicare, and waiting until 66 or later for full Social Security benefits — which today average just $1,335 per person.

With our retirement funds held in IRAs invested in stocks and mutual funds, 25% of baby boomers saw their life savings wiped out during the recession of 2007–2009. We need to return to productive employment to restock our retirement piggy banks if we have any hope of surviving financially during our retirement years.

Our generation is doing what previous generations have not done. We are demanding to remain in the workforce long after employees our age traditionally retired and died. While the ADEA Act of 1976 mandates that we not be discriminated against due to age, the challenge is to overcome the cultural prejudice and lack of effective role models to persuade employers that we, as a generation, are outstanding employees that need to be a vital part of the workforce today. We will tackle those arguments next.

DOES AGE DISCRIMINATION REALLY EXIST IN AMERICA TODAY?

If you are currently well employed, you are lucky. Work hard to keep that job, as it will be difficult to find another one should you lose it for any reason.

If you are part of the legion of the unemployed, the statistics are terrifying.

Ageism Exists — and Here's Proof

There's a good chance that age will hurt your job prospects, especially if you're in your 50s or older, based on a recent Federal Reserve Bank of San Francisco study. Researchers created realistic, but fictitious, résumés for job seekers who are young (aged 29 to 31), middle-aged (49 to 51), and older (64 to 66) and sent out more than 40,000 applications for over 13,000 low-skill positions in 12 cities. Older applicants, particularly older *female* applicants, were much less likely to be contacted for interviews; in some fields, as much as 47% less likely.

A 2013 AARP study found that almost two in three workers ages 45 to 74 reported experiencing age discrimination in the workplace.

Ageism is definitely alive and well in Corporate America. Here's more information to consider:

There's A Growing Legion Of Long-Term Unemployed Due To Job Displacement

+ Of the 3.2 million workers displaced from jobs they had held for 3 or more years (2013–2015), 34% remained unemployed long term (BLS 8/24/16).
+ The June 2017 unemployment rate for workers seeking employment was 3.2% for those over 55, but does not reflect the large numbers who abandoned their job search.

Employees Over 50 Have A Much Harder Time Finding A New Job When They Lose Their Old One

+ Of those not re-employed, older workers fared worse: 40% of workers aged 55–64, and 63% of workers 65 plus were not re-employed, compared to just 37% of workers aged 25–54 (BLS 8/24/16)
+ It takes boomers almost twice as long to find a job as a younger worker. In the 2014 Displaced Worker Survey, researchers found the odds of being re-employed decrease by 2.6% for each one-year increase in age.
+ According to AARP, the average length of time it took seniors to find a job was about 55 weeks. Those under age 55 averaged 28 weeks — half as long.
+ Federal Reserve economists interviewed by CNN estimated that only one in ten job seekers per month find work after a year or more of unemployment.
+ The average professional career job search takes six to twenty-four months, per author Marc Miller.

When Baby Boomers Do Find Jobs, Half Are Hired At A Lower Pay Level

+ Of the 66% of unemployed baby boomers that did find jobs, almost half (47%) received salaries below their prior compensation level (BLS 8/24/16)
+ According to U.S. Department of Labor's Chief Economist, Heidi Shierholz, workers between the ages of 54 and 65 earned 13.5 percent less in a new job after being unemployed for any reason.

Boomers Plan to Work Later — If They Can Find Jobs

In coming decades, the share of seniors age 65 and older in the U.S. working-age population is projected to rise sharply — from about 19% currently to 29% in the year 2060 — approaching equality with the shares of those aged 25–44 and 45–64, according to AARP.

Boomers NEED to Work Longer

A survey released in 2017 by the Public Policy Institute of AARP found a quarter of Americans 50 years and older used up all their savings during the 2007–2009 recession. The study also found that 55% of the long-term unemployed say they will need to retire later than planned because of the recession, while five percent say the weak economy forced them into early retirement.

Most of us are waiting eagerly to hit 62 so we can start collecting Social Security reduced benefits, or age 66 to collect full Social Security benefits, and that blessing of all blessings, Medicare at 65. Only at that age do most of us have enough of a safety net that we don't risk imminent bankruptcy from long-term unemployment or a serious uninsured medical emergency. According to a recent Harvard Study, 62% of all personal bankruptcies were due to unanticipated medical expenses and this was despite the fact that 72% of those bankrupt individuals had medical insurance. According to a 2010 report on *CBSnews.com*, the average cost of a heart attack was $760,000. There is practically no way an uninsured person could survive the financial devastation of a major health crisis like a heart attack, stroke or cancer.

Even the medical deductibles from many plans today can wipe out a family's lifetime savings in a period of just a couple of months. When combined with lack of a salary, older workers are tapped out financially by one single illness.

Even supporting an ill mate or parent can send you spiraling towards destitution. Private care in a nursing home averages $81,000 per year, according to *Sapling.com*, while Alzheimer's care facilities cost between $5,000 and $8,500 a month. If you are under 65, you must become destitute to be eligible for government-provided care, known as Medicaid, so any assets you have must be totally depleted before the government steps up. Many couples have been forced to divorce so that the ill partner can get much-needed medical care. This is the number one reason many older adults live together rather than marry.

So, as a practical matter, baby boomers today need to work at least to age 65 until they qualify for Medicare.

Just as importantly, who wants to stop being productive? Hemmingway proclaimed that "Retirement is the ugliest word in the English language." Malcolm Forbes declared that "Retirement kills more people than hard work ever did."

So maybe we need to redefine what "retirement" is today in light of recent market and demographic shifts. And it may not be what you considered in the past. As a group, let's redefine retirement.

Perhaps it's time to find ways to work longer and more enjoyably, transition into a slower pace, do what you are passionate about, or just change your life all together.

The good news? This book is your roadmap to success in reinventing your life and career to overcome these many hurdles and find meaningful and productive employment or engagement for as long as you want to work.

3

BUT ISN'T AGE DISCRIMINATION AGAINST THE LAW?

Surprised to learn there is so much age discrimination in the work place today? I was. After all, it's been 50 years — half a CENTURY — since the federal Age Discrimination in Employment Act (ADEA) of 1967 became law.

Mind you, there was much more blatant and egregious age discrimination practiced way back then, when the average life span was much lower, and employers assumed that older workers were unfit to hold jobs. Many companies had mandatory retirement at age 65 or after 30 years of employment, whichever came first. And they used a whole host of blatantly unfair practices to restrict older employees' hiring and promotion.

But the ADEA set out to change all that and did make a dramatic difference in age discrimination.

The ADEA states:

> It shall be unlawful for an employer (1) to fail or refuse to hire or to discharge any individual or otherwise discriminate against any individual with respect to his compensation, terms, conditions, or privileges of employment, because of such individual's age . . . [or] (2) to limit, segregate, or classify his employees in any way which would deprive or tend to deprive any individual of employment opportunities or otherwise adversely affect his status as an employee, because of such individual's age.

Over the years, the ADEA has been augmented to include benefit plan discrimination (ERISA), and has had many cases tried throughout courts all the way to the US Supreme Court. However, employers can intentionally or inadvertently discriminate against hiring and promoting older employees, in part by new and emerging technologies which allow the hyper-targeting of ads and messages based on a number of different criteria, including age.

On March 27, 2017, NPR carried a story documenting rampant age discrimination: *Older Workers Find Age Discrimination Built Right In To Some Job Websites*. Journalist Ina Jaffe reported that some job sites were building discrimination into their résumé building tools. "The Illinois Attorney General opened an investigation after a 70-year-old man called her office and complained that he'd been unable to use a résumé building tool on a job search site, because the dates on the drop-down menu that required you to select the year when you graduated or got your first job only went back to 1980, which effectively excluded anyone over 52." The Attorney General's investigation prompted most job search sites to change the date range for college degrees or limit the number of years of job history they reported, but this is still a reflection on the mentality of the younger workers who run and manage tech sites like these.

According to an investigation led by *ProPublica* and the *New York Times* a few months later, and reported in *Salon.com*, "Companies like Verizon, Amazon, Goldman Sachs, Target, and Facebook have reportedly targeted specific job ads to limited age groups...which have many questioning if this practice is a violation of the federal Age Discrimination in Employment Act of 1967."

The report adds, "Facebook has, of course, defended the practice, which uses the social media platform's ability to target people by location, age, gender and interests."

According to Rob Goldman, Facebook's VP of Ads, in a statement released online, "US law forbids discrimination in employment based on age, race, gender and other legally protected characteristics. That said, simply showing certain job ads to different age groups on services like Facebook or Google may not in itself be discriminatory — just as it can be okay to run employment ads in magazines and on TV shows targeted at younger or older people."

But on Dec. 20, 2017, the Communications Workers of America (CWA), filed a class action lawsuit against T-Mobile US, Amazon, Cox Communications and Media Group, and hundreds of other large employers who have allegedly been engaging in this discriminatory practice, according to Nicole Karlis, a news writer at *Salon.com*.

"This pattern or practice of discrimination denies job opportunities to individuals who are searching for and interested in jobs, reduces the number of older workers who apply for jobs with the offending employers and employment agencies, and depresses the number of older workers who are hired by such employers and employment agencies, causing working families to lose out on wages, benefits, and the dignity that comes with a good job."

Facebook's rebuttal letter closes with this statement: "Used responsibly, age-based targeting for employment purposes is an accepted industry practice and for good reason: it helps employers recruit and help people of all ages find work."

Ageism and age discrimination exist. It is often subtle. But it is a cause for concern, and more importantly, attention. In this book, you will learn ways to counter that discrimination with tools that lessen or eradicate the impact of age on your career outlook and find ways to turn those many years of experience into an asset rather than a liability.

4

SO WHY DO COMPANIES PREFER MILLENNIALS OVER BABY BOOMERS TODAY?

We know that companies are hiring younger workers over older workers, but WHY?

Only by learning the reasons employers prefer younger workers will we acquire the tools to fight back.

We often want to feel like the victim, treated unfairly by big bad corporations for no reason. But there are a number of very valid reasons for this trend. It helps us plan our employment strategies if we understand what they are, whether real or perceived. Only then can we craft effective strategies to neutralize these perceived deficits and highlight our true strengths so our age can be seen as an asset (or at least a non-issue) rather than a liability.

There are 4 key reasons companies are hiring millennials instead of boomers:

1. They cost less — the obvious reason
2. They are technologically savvy — the key reason
3. The way companies work has change — a result of the age shift
4. The physical workplace has changed — another key trend

Let's explore each reason so you better understand the thought processes and can craft your message to overcome the issue.

1. Higher Costs for Baby Boomers than Millennials

As a general rule, baby boomers cost a company more than younger workers in the same job, and the increased costs come from several different areas:

Base Salaries

It's true that many large companies compete actively for a handful of high-potential talent, recruiting the best engineers, architects, lawyers, and consultants at exorbitant salaries during key college recruiting periods at prestigious universities. But most of us aren't competing with those high-pressure superstars in their unique niches. Only about 20% of new college grads have jobs to start on the Monday after they walk the stage to receive their diplomas. That means that of three million new college grads each year, 2.4 million are unemployed and competing for entry level jobs with salaries in the range of $20,000 to $30,000. It's easy to see that an employer will seek ways to transfer workload from a $50,000 per year middle manager to a newly-minted grad at $25,000 or $30,000 whenever possible.

Cost of Medical Insurance Premiums

Another key issue is the rapidly-increasing cost of medical insurance provided by companies. A few years ago, I was responsible for administering our company group insurance. We had a small company, with 2 key execs in their 60s, and more than a dozen young hourly workers. I struggled to find adequate insurance that was affordable. I discovered that many group medical policies are age-rated, and policies for young workers in their 20s averaged between $150 and $250 per month — even for women in an age bracket where they can be expected to have babies which will be paid for by the group medical policy. However, policies for workers in their 60s frequently cost between $1,200 and $1,500 per month, up to 6 times more for basic group medical insurance premiums.

Since then, Obamacare mandated that the premium be no more than three times higher for older workers than younger employees. But with the dramatic change in insurance plans with huge deductibles and skyrocketing premiums, this is still a major cost consideration.

With the move to repeal and replace Obamacare, the guidelines on medical insurance premiums are up in the air, and they continue to be a significant concern for employers.

Higher Usage of Medical Benefits

Older workers tend to have more severe medical issues than younger employees and have a much higher incidence of age-related illnesses like cancer, heart attacks, strokes, and diabetes. Treatment for these conditions can be astronomically expensive, often up to $1,000,000 per heart attack, aggressive cancer treatment, or organ transplant. Pricing for a company's insurance plan takes into account the claims from the prior year, so these catastrophic illnesses will drive up the group medical cost of the following year.

Higher Disability Insurance Costs

Older workers who have these severe medical conditions are often placed first on short-term and then long-term disability, adding more costs to an employer's benefit plan. Again, disability costs are averaged each year, and policy rates increase as a function of the amount of the claims.

More Vacation Time

Traditionally, vacation and paid time off were based on years of employment. Employees received two weeks of paid vacation during their first five years of employment, three weeks for five to ten years, and up to four or five weeks for long-term employees. This increased paid time off can equate to a difference of up to a month (or eight percent of total annual pay) between a new hire and a long-tenured worker. Again, it can really add up for an employer who is paying an onerous 35% of total salaries in fringe benefits. Today, employers are shifting to a lump-sum of 10 to 15 days for total PTO — Paid Time Off — which includes vacation, sick days and personal days. But longer-employed workers are generally grandfathered in to more vacation time, which yields a higher cost.

2. Millennials are More Tech Savvy

Perhaps the number one reason baby boomers are losing in the employment race is the widening technology gap. Baby boomers are digital immigrants, having to adopt technology which can seem foreign. Younger workers are digital natives, born practically clutching a smart phone or iPad. Plus digital technology is growing exponentially, doubling every two years.

Modest improvement in skills may not keep up with the rapidly-widening gap between how different generations use technology.

We grew up playing outside and honed gross motor skills as children — playing sports, tossing balls, swinging bats, riding bicycles, swimming and diving, walking and running. Millennials grew up in an inside environment entertained by video games and online role-playing games, using fine motor skills, focused intently on a digital screen. They are trained to act and react quickly by clicking buttons and pushing joy sticks, living a reactionary life inundated constantly by digital stimuli. They have mastered speed typing on two-inch phone screens using just their thumbs, while many baby boomers struggle to send a simple text message. At the same time, millenials have a hard time holding a pen or pencil and most can't write in cursive.

Older workers are being increasingly disenfranchised as employers embrace workers who bring digital skills to the table. But we can compete. All it takes is to steadfastly and constantly seek to increase our computer skills. However, many companies assume all new employees have those in-demand skills and don't offer training to help older workers catch up.

Word, Excel and PowerPoint are bare minimums for employment today, and many employers expect much more. Companies are shifting to cloud storage of documents, online collaboration, real-time editing of shared documents in the cloud, and a whole host of collaborative apps that make work easier, faster, more democratic and more efficient — once you know how to use them.

As an example, six months ago I had never heard of a mobile app called Slack, which allows for instantaneous team sharing of short content similar to text messages. Within three months, four different companies or organizations I was affiliated with adopted Slack — showing how fast new programs and applications are springing up, or becoming obsolete.

Static knowledge of a couple of programs just isn't enough to stay relevant in today's job market. My 29-year-old son Alex worked in a high tech company and said he was online the whole time he was at work, using on average 10 different computer programs or apps throughout the day.

If you are apprehensive, don't despair. In future chapters we will explore ways you can bridge this digital technology gap and find a number of resources to help you "Tech UP"!

3. How Companies Work is Changing Dramatically

Over the past few years, more and more businesses have adopted the characteristics of America's superstar companies — the tech giants from Silicon Valley. These rapidly-growing companies, filled with young tech-savvy employees on the cutting edge of the digital revolution, have transformed Corporate America's view of how businesses should operate.

To compete, companies are rapidly evolving to be lean, agile, flatter organizations. They are redefining corporate leadership, adding key roles like Chief Technology Officer, VP of Customer Retention, Customer Journey Officer, Lead Nurturing Specialist, Customer Evangelist, Pipeline Specialist, Community Manager, and more.

Coca-Cola recently shocked the marketing community when it announced that it had eliminated the sacrosanct title of CMO — Chief Marketing Officer — and replaced it with a Chief Growth Officer. It was such a big deal that Advertising Age, the primary publication of the advertising industry, made it a leading article.

The traditional pyramid-style organization chart is evolving to Agile or Scrum teamwork models with shared responsibilities which define the changed process methods used to achieve a goal today. They replace strict "waterfall" planning processes with more flexible planning, frequent iterations, welcome course correction, beta testing, and customer/developer collaboration.

As an example, workers at USAA are grouped in teams of 10 or 12, and each self-organizing team defines its specific goals and action plan for the next two weeks. If one team member fails to deliver, other team members are required to fill the void so the team as a whole meets its goals. At the end of each two-week period, the team reassembles with the supervisor, team members review what was accomplished, what was learned, what worked or didn't work, and then the group creates its next set of two-week goals.

Just one year ago, all this sounded like Greek to me. I realized that I had to become more aware of what is going on in the wider world of work. I am living proof that you, too, can adapt to changes and adopt new skills to stay relevant. More importantly, once you openly accept these new ways of work, you avoid being labeled outdated, not a team player, too old or too old fashioned to remain part of the team.

4. The Physical Workplace Is Changing

Corporate workplaces are changing, and millenials are driving that transformation. Companies love it because they are reducing costs dramatically.

The long-coveted corner office has often been converted into a conference room or a shared workspace filled with work stations where anyone can sit, plug in their laptop and start to work. Smaller "huddle rooms" are set up for small meetings, and "phone rooms" may not even provide a place to sit, as so many people prefer to pace while talking on their mobile phones.

Many companies issue mobile phones to their employees and can forward calls to a supervisor or co-worker the moment the employee leaves the job so no business leads are lost. In some companies which still require employees to come to an office, they may have an extension that rings to whatever phone they log onto when sitting down to work, or calls are forwarded to their mobile phone.

Today, many companies are questioning whether they need a physical office, and often the answer is "no." Rapidly-evolving technology has allowed workers to perform their jobs from anywhere they can access a mobile phone and laptop, so the thought of paying thousands of dollars each month to house a local 10-person sales office looks untenable. As a result, thousands of companies are reassigning their employees to work from home offices with company-provided laptops, printers and mobile phones. If you are a front-line employee, such as sales or customer service, you may soon find yourself working from your home office in your bunny slippers. However, if you are in an administrative role, such as office manager or administrative assistant, your job may disappear when the office closes its doors. With so many companies shifting to home offices, you may not easily find another administrative position, which is one of the reasons I wrote this book.

Tech incubators are springing up around the country, and shared workspace buildings are everywhere, offering a range of plans as low as $50 per month to several hundred for the opportunity to work in a safe, comfortable, 24/7 open space environment. Rental rates vary based on the real estate market, but the lowered cost of shared workspace everywhere is rapidly transforming businesses.

"Members" of these flexible workplace facilities enjoy the use of shared facilities such as conference rooms, small meeting rooms, video conferencing, large screen monitors scattered throughout the building, a fully equipped snack room with free sodas, coffee, snacks, even beer and wine at times, and other refreshments all day long. These new office suites often come with wireless high-speed internet throughout, mailboxes for an "office address", package reception, access to a copy machine or shared printer, and a receptionist to greet visitors and answer and forward phone calls to the member's mobile phone seamlessly. They often offer pleasant seating and conversation areas both inside and outside on a patio or deck, so all you need is your laptop to work anywhere you wish.

Many of these facilitates require no annual contract, and you pay as you go one month at a time. You can also choose to rent a traditional office with furniture, file cabinets and a locking door for less than $1,000 a month, with all utilities provided, in San Antonio today.

Importantly, these shared-use facilities aren't just for start-ups and entrepreneurial firms. A whole host of Fortune 500 companies rent such shared space offices around the country to provide quality meeting rooms for their local sales teams who now work from their home.

I spent several hours with Luis Escobar, owner of Venture Point, which he describes as a Business Hub for Mobile Entrepreneurs (*www.VenturePointSA.com*). Luis operates two large shared space facilities (often called "collaborative workplaces") in San Antonio with more than 350 clients. I was amazed by the list of blue chip companies which had contracts for space in his buildings. He shared the surprising stats that companies or individuals leasing a shared space averaged just two and one half hours per week usage of the facilities.

These changes are dramatically different from the way we started our careers, but it is the new normal for millenials, who had similar experiences in their recent college years.

According to *Wired.com*, this trend will continue, with 63 million people — 43% of all US workers — currently working from home offices,

We baby boomers need to welcome and embrace these changes, rather than fight against them. I, for one, am much happier working from home rather than getting dressed up in a suit and high heels. I save a lot on makeup, and the time and money I save not commuting to an office is an added bonus.

In another way, it's a huge advantage for us to work from home, because colleagues and clients can't see us to put us in the "too old" box.

To understand the phenomenon of the changing workplace, I highly recommend that you watch two fairly recent and very funny movies with similar titles:

- *The Internship* — 2013 — with Owen Wilson and Vince Vaughn — set in part at Google's headquarters in Silicon Valley, so the physical environment is real and not Hollywood fiction.
- *The Intern* — 2015 — with Robert De Niro and Anne Hathaway. The movie portrays an online clothing start up in a major city, which is now housed in the office where De Nero managed a phone book printing business for 40 years until it went out of business.

You may want to watch both movies several times, to look beyond the outrageously funny antics to study the workplace environment and culture to see where work in America is headed. Imagine what it would be like to work in those environments, and "try them on for size", in your imagination.

The changes in the workplace today are sudden, severe and dramatic, and can be off-putting to those of us who grew up working in traditional Corporate America offices. Complaining and nay-saying can be a death knell to your career if overheard and negative feelings may be transmitted through your body language, posture and facial expressions in unguarded moments. So bite the bullet and look forward to a new adventure.

5

TEN REASONS THEY SHOULD HIRE YOU INSTEAD OF A MILLENNIAL

We just saw a lot of reasons why Corporate America prefers to hire younger workers. It can be challenging and disheartening.

But on the flip side, there are very good reasons they should be hiring baby boomers instead. It is our responsibility to showcase them in our interactions with the job market at all times. Why not learn to play to our strengths, rather than give up due to our perceived weaknesses?

The ten most important reasons that baby boomers are critical to the success of businesses and organizations today — and in the future — include:

1. Company and Industry Experience
2. Strong Work Ethic
3. Reliability and Stability
4. Communication Skills
5. Dedication and Loyalty
6. Wisdom and Judgment—Gut Feeling
7. Mentoring Ability
8. Extensive Personal and Professional Network
9. Flexibility and Adaptability
10. The Value of Money

We will review each of these in detail, and provide potential scripts you can use in interviews and job applications, to showcase these strengths.

1. Company and Industry History

You bring a unique and much-needed perspective to your employer. In the role of the industry historian, you provide a knowledge base of how the industry has evolved and can help avoid mistakes made in the past. As Edmund Burke said, "Those who don't know history are doomed to repeat it."

Couch this insight in a positive light: you contribute knowledge and expertise to new ideas brought to the table by industry novices. Your goal should be to become the company go-to source for information, data, insights, and suggestions.

That puts you into any project as the bearer of valuable knowledge. Soon, the new rising stars will ask your opinion before they risk their reputation recommending an un-vetted idea. Senior management will refer newer employees to check with you before wasting time and energy on a questionable project.

During an interview, you can position your experience positively by saying, *"I have X years in this industry (or company, or field), and I can provide valuable insight into the challenges the industry (or company) has addressed, both successfully and not so successfully, and provide insight into where we might be heading given those changes."* Don't get stuck in the past. Showcase this experience in a forward-looking manner, and let the interviewer envision the positive contributions you can make.

2. Work Ethic

We have what so many younger workers may not have — a strong work ethic. We know what commitments, deadlines and obligations are all about. We know it may not be fun, stimulating, challenging, or pleasant work. But if it has to be done, we do it, especially if no one else is willing to step up to the table. We are committed to completing whatever project, work or challenge we say we will do, and will honor our commitments over the long haul. We aren't seeking a promotion or the next opportunity every six months.

That may make us appear staid, unexciting, or boring. However, we are the unsung heroes of a company. We are responsible for keeping the train running smoothly on the tracks, arriving and departing on time, with supplies arriving unannounced, with the toilets and staterooms clean, and the ticket taker and engineer in place and able to do their jobs unhindered by last minute problems (please forgive the metaphor.)

This is an important point for employers. Highlight this trait gracefully. Mention your strong work ethic in your résumé and in job interviews. Tell quick anecdotes of a time you quietly intervened to prevent a disaster, stayed all night to assemble the sales materials for the product launch the next day, or stepped in to temporarily take over another department or job when the responsible employee was unexpectedly hospitalized or quit without notice.

3. Reliability and Stability

You bring valuable skills and habits that can be overlooked when a recruiter is blinded by flashy young talent.

Your boss knows he can rely on you to arrive at an important meeting on time, bring the right materials or presentations, dress professionally, and interact in an appropriate manner to represent your company well. You've been trained and tested many times to be a proven asset. Your supervisor can pair you with the new younger hot shot employee to show him the ropes, make introductions, provide continuity of contact, and guide the meeting based on prior knowledge of the participants and topics.

To keep your job, remind your supervisor of this, especially in light of the rapid turnover of millenials and early-career professionals who tend to job hop frequently, both as a function of seeking rapid promotions as well as sorting out where they want to be career-wise.

My millennial son explained that his generation has learned that you can earn a 30% pay increase by job hopping every year or two, as compared to just a three to five percent annual pay increase if you stay put. His peers consider this an employer problem, and that companies are taking advantage of their stable employees. He stated that his peers have become mercenaries, and feel that employees who stays around in a job or company for very long are considered to be "suckers." Turnover is a key concern for an employer, so your emphasis on reliability and stability can be a key attribute in your favor.

During an interview, showcase these traits with statements like *"I've worked for XYZ for 10 years, with positions of progressive responsibility. I have forged strong relationships with key clients, who depend on me to know their needs and wants and provide reliable support despite many changes in operating procedures and support staff over the years. I look forward to providing your customers with the same reliable service and support."* Again, keep it forward-looking, and help the recruiter or interviewer envision you as providing that excellent and consistent service for their company.

On your résumé, you will show either your employment dates for each company, or the number of years you worked for the employer. You may want to list dates for each key position to show steady progression. Also, it is a good idea to list awards and recognitions which showcase excellent and reliable behavior. Consider adding a statement like *"20 years of steady career progression, with consistently excellent reviews by supervisors and clients."*

4. Communication Skills

We grew up in a world where grammar and spelling were critical skills, driven into our heads by years of diagramming sentences, spelling quizzes, and learning parts of speech in English classes. If we failed the class, we had to repeat it until we mastered perfect grammar, punctuation, spelling and enunciation. We learned to shake hands politely when we were practically toddlers, and "yes ma'am" and "please" and "thank you" were drilled into our heads at an early age.

These written and verbal skills are important to our employers, because they reflect on the company's image when we interact with the public or key stakeholders. As a generation, we can communicate in writing and speech more effectively than many millenials, who grew up communicating in 140-character tweets, emoticons, and abbreviated text messages where U, LOL and countless other abbreviations are frequently used.

When I worked in media sales at Valassis, I called on one customer who shared how offended she was to get email messages from a young sales rep for a competitor with text-like spelling and grammar. Needless to say, I got the business. This is especially true if you are communicating with mature individuals in your job.

Workplace communication style is changing due to the prominence of millenials, and today communication is leaner, more condensed, and less flowery. We'll talk about that in a future chapter. But it is important to highlight communication excellence in seeking to land a new job.

During an interview, you might want to say something like *"I have become the informal gatekeeper for all written communication to top management. I am tasked to proofread and wordsmith key letters, ad copy and proposals."* This is a reminder of another way you add value that a recruiter or hiring manager may not have thought of.

5. Dedication and Loyalty

Millennials are infamous for job hopping, many staying with companies for less than a year before moving on to another opportunity. A number of employers complain that younger workers show little loyalty to the company, and don't "wear the company uniform" like older employees do.

Show long periods of employment for the same company on your résumé or have very good and understandable reasons for shorter-term work. Acceptable explanations for frequent job shifts might be:

- *"My husband has just retired from the Air Force, and I am looking forward to staying in one place and working for one company, for a long period of time. My employers always knew we were on assignment and valued my contributions during our time in that market, but my promotions were limited by the expectation we would be moving within a given period of time. I'd love to show you the outstanding letters of recommendation I received from my former supervisors."*

- *"Three years ago, I made the painful choice to leave my long-time employer and a job I loved to move to XYZ city to take care of my aging mother with Alzheimer's. She has since passed on, and I am looking forward to re-starting my career without the limitations those family obligations caused."*

- *"Two years ago, my division was eliminated in a dramatic downsizing, and I lost my job along with 47 other colleagues. I don't like taking handouts, so I took a job at XYZ company at a pay rate far below my prior salary, rather than spend a year sitting in the unemployment office. At the time, I discussed with my employer that I would be looking for a higher-level job long-term, but we agreed that my skills fit a unique need the company had at that time. I've worked in that less-challenging position gratefully and brought my world-class skills to help build out the department, so that the company will be in a much stronger position when it is my time to move back to my desired functional area. My supervisor knows I will be looking for a position in this field and gives me flexible time for interviews, and we've agreed that I will give the company up to a full month notice to adequately train my replacement."*

- *"My industry overall has been in a transition, and I had the awful experience of losing my job twice in a row due to downsizing. It has been painful to me, as I am extremely loyal as an employee, but nothing could be done to salvage the situation for my employers, who were both hit by the 2008 recession, and the rapid technological transformation of the industry. I actually stayed on as the last employee at XYZ company and took on the responsibility of closing down the office, disposing of equipment, shredding documents, cancelling contracts and services, and helping my colleagues transition to the best of everyone's ability."*

- *"I left an outstanding job at XYZ company to join the very lean management team of a new start up in the XYZ industry. Despite early success, the company floundered when an investor failed to make the equity contributions he had agreed to due to his own personal financial problem, and the company was forced to close. I lost the value of my stock options, but I learned a huge amount about start-ups, business management, budgeting, planning and operations that will serve me and my future employer in my next assignment."*

With any explanation, look to add a favorable spin to what this means to your future employer — loyalty, work ethic, values, learning of new skills, valuable new insights, ways you contributed during the transition, etc. Think of how your employer will react to your explanation. You want them to walk away thinking, *"She had some bad luck, but she sure is the kind of a person I want on my team."*

6. Extensive Personal and Professional Network

One of the most overlooked benefits you bring to an employer is the strong personal and professional network built over several decades. Many of the people you started out with are now in positions of great responsibility or influence in your industry, which can be an asset to your employer (as well as to you in your job search.) Ask them to write you a letter of recommendation, endorse and recommend you on LinkedIn, or serve as a reference. They are industry insiders and can let you know about new business opportunities, trends, or make introductions to potential clients or employers.

Actively build your professional network every day regardless of whether or not you anticipate losing your job or making a career change. It's just good business to take care of your reputation and build your network.

Your network is who you know. Your reputation is how you are known to others. Focus on connecting with as many people as possible, at all times. That includes volunteer activities and professional association participation. You want to be visible to industry insiders and influencers, so seek opportunities to present at professional organizations, trade shows, conferences, industry association luncheons, and more.

Read more on this topic in my book *BRAND YOU! To Land Your Dream Job*, Section 3 — *Network Your Way to Career Success*. It is available from Amazon and my website *www.BrandYouGuide.com*. We will also be discussing how to network effectively in a future chapter.

7. Wisdom, Judgement, and Gut Feeling

Wisdom and good judgment are great assets you bring to your employer. You know the saying, "Success comes from wisdom, and wisdom comes from experience." Einstein said "Wisdom is not a product of schooling, but of a life-long attempt to acquire it." Equally relevant is the adage "To be old and wise, you must first be young and stupid." Experience fuels your intuitive judgment, which younger workers simply don't have.

A related intangible is "gut feeling", also referred to as intuition. I have engaged in discussions with others in my field, and we agree that the unique experience of having "gut feeling" about business or your profession often takes eight to ten years or longer to develop. Gut feeling is your subconscious tapping into a host of information and experiences to create a quick intuitive judgment that bypasses the conscious thought process. At our age, we know not to ignore that sinking feeling in our stomach when something isn't right, that uneasiness when something feels off, and the quickening solid feeling when a decision is right. Remember "Always trust your gut. It knows what your head hasn't figured out yet."

During a salary review in your current job, or in a job interview, you might remind your interviewer, *"I've been in this industry (or company, or job) for X years, and I have seen a lot of successes and failures. I've been fortunate to learn what has impacted both outcomes. I may not always have the right solution, but I do know a lot of things to avoid. And I can rely on my gut feeling to steer me away from the disasters."*

8. Mentoring Ability

Our experience and wisdom allow us the insight to teach others with confidence and grace. We're generally parents, and often grandparents, and have developed the aptitude to teach, mentor and counsel in a loving, helpful and constructive manner. With the right attitude, we can help train the future generation in our company without feeling threatened. This is a key trait that employers value, and makes you stand out over younger employees.

You can drive this point home in an interview by statements such as, "*I enjoy mentoring others in the industry, and taking some of our younger or less confident colleagues under my wing to help them navigate the organization.*" Or, "*I have become the department 'go to' person to help guide younger colleagues through the complex corporate hierarchy. And I thoroughly enjoy it; I often learn valuable insights or skills from people I mentor.*" Emphasize that younger workers make you feel valued for your knowledge, and your willingness to share it freely with them.

9. Flexibility and Adaptability

We have seen a lot, experienced a lot, and made incredible changes in our lives and careers. We watched the debut of Macintosh on Super Bowl Sunday in 1984 and remember when the first McDonalds or Wal-Mart came to town. We grew into our professions before personal computers, the internet, broadband, mobile phones, accounting software, electronic calculators, even before fax machines. Our generation INVENTED them all!

We worked in companies like the agency of "Mad Men" and organizations like NASA during the segregation days of "Hidden Figures" and "Selma" and encountered racial, gender and age discrimination unheard of today. We put the first man on the moon and invented how to do it!

We survived and some of us even thrived during upheavals in business structure, government, legislation, the economy, education, culture, immigration and so much more. We suffered through 14% mortgage rates during the days of Jimmy Carter, endured runaway inflation and price controls under Richard Nixon, lost our businesses and jobs and dreams in the dotcom crash of 2001, and again in 2008.

The steel of our spines has been tempered by huge, rapid-fire changes in the past, and we will weather them in the future. We are resilient and have shown our resiliency over decades. We're not going to quit now. We are going to do what we have always done — adapting and changing, keeping up with exponential technological transformation and reinvention of the workplace. You can emphasize this during a job interview, with statements like: *"I've been in this industry for X years, and I've seen many dramatic changes that threatened our company and livelihood. But we've adapted and become stronger for the experience. As we go forward, I'll be able to use the insights of what we've already experienced to provide a point of reference for future changes."* Again, mention how your understanding of the past will benefit your employer in the future.

10. The Value of Money

We grew up in a world of working hard for our money, saving to get what we want, living frugally whenever possible, and investing in things that will give us a return — whether it's an education we worked to pay for, a family car so we can get to work, our first home with that terrifying mortgage, or our IRA and investment portfolio.

Today's millenials grew up with $150,000 tuition costs, $37,000 average student debt over and above what mom and dad paid, and $30,000 cars in their high school parking lot. When they marry they will spend $30,000 or more for a wedding, $5,000 for the wedding dress alone.

Most of them have never paid income taxes before getting out of college, don't understand that Uncle Sam is taking 10% out of their paychecks for the rest of their lives to pay for Social Security and Medicare, and have no concept that their employer is paying another 10% matching contribution to Uncle Sam on their behalf. Many of them will be shocked when they get their first paycheck and see all the deductions.

They are also in for a shock when they have to finance their own car, try to pull together $35,000 down payment for their first house, or start paying more than $700 per month per child for daycare.

So when they start on the new job, they may not have the perspective to understand department budgets, sales forecasts, financial limitations, P&Ls, travel policies, and more. They may not yet have the financial maturity to understand the big numbers and perspectives of business and industry, and how the little costs build up and have to be controlled.

You may want to mention something like, "*I am very aware of the budgetary constraints of a publicly-traded company, and how important it is to manage spending, while delivering on revenue and profit projections.*" Since an interviewer is unlikely to hear from that from a Millennial, it will reinforce your business maturity.

Embrace the Role of the Old Backup Quarterback

Unless you are firmly entrenched in a top-level position in your current company, it may not be realistic to think that you will become the CEO or suddenly become a company rock star. At our age, we may need to be realistic and step back to let the new young superstars shine. But we still have great value to a company. Think of your favorite football team. There's a young hard-charging quarterback who takes all the hits on Sunday and earns top dollar for the privilege. Our role should be that of the experienced backup quarterback, to shore up the team with wisdom, coaching and perspective, while being on call to step in and hold things together in the case of an emergency. It's an important role and we should understand the value we have for the organization. We still have to show up to practice every day, get in uniform, even if we just sit on the bench most of the season. But we are the team insurance policy, experienced and knowledgeable about the game, and able to do a decent job at a moment's notice to save the day and stave off disaster. We may not lead our team into the playoffs, but we can help the team hold onto our ranking until the superstar recovers from a sprained ankle or broken toe. Even though it feels great to play again, do you really want to take all those hits at this stage and age? If you can embrace this new role, you add value to the company, and will enjoy your work a lot more.

HOW TO KEEP OR LAND A JOB IN CORPORATE AMERICA

As we age, we need to stay relevant to the changing workplace. But often we focus so much on doing our jobs, living our lives, and raising our families that we forget to market ourselves within the company, much less outside in the industry. If you want to stay employed, get a promotion, find a new job, or re-enter the workforce, you need to address four additional areas that will help you stay relevant and erase the perceived age disadvantage:

1. **Tech Up!** — Embrace technology and actively seek out new skills to close the technology divide
2. **Embrace Life Long Learning** — Your job and company are evolving daily, and learning skills in addition to computer technology will keep you relevant and worthy of promotions
3. **Look and Act As Young As You Can Without Looking Silly** — It's time for a head-to-toe makeover to erase decades from your appearance
4. **Adopt Younger Actions and Habits** — Learn to embrace and implement subtle behaviors that will bridge the age gap

Read on…there's a lot to learn in this chapter that will make all the difference in keeping or losing your job due to age.

6

TECH UP!

The key reason your job may be at risk is a lack of current technology skills. To improve your employability, actively seek out, embrace, and master computer and technology skills.

Bridge the Technology Divide

Many of us baby boomers learned our key job skills before the PC existed, and long before software was invented. When I was earning my MBA in the 70's, I took my first computer programming class. My team was issued a stack of manila key punch cards, and we spent the semester learning to program a simple mathematical formula. That was the state of the art of computers in the 70's, and many baby boomers never even had that experience. As a result, today's rapidly-evolving technology is new, foreign, and often uncomfortable to baby boomers — and for very good reason. Those of us who learned to use a computer during the days of DOS and <C (C-prompt) recognized back then that this was not going to be easy — and it wasn't.

Younger workers grew up with plug-and-play PCs loaded with easy-to-use software and scores of video games in their bedrooms while they were still in elementary school. They are digital natives, fluent in many aspects of technology, while our generation is comprised of digital immigrants, many unable or unwilling to speak the language, or who speak technology with a heavy accent (metaphorically speaking).

The good news is that basic computer technology today is much simpler than in the days of DOS, memorizing formulas and writing our own basic programs. So stop being intimidated by technology and embrace it whole-heartedly as key to your future success.

Surprisingly, many companies assume you know a host of programs, and don't offer training on computers. More than 12 years ago, I worked for a $3 billion media sales organization, with more than 250 sales representatives.

We had to prepare beautiful presentations, write persuasive proposals, and manipulate complex databases with thousands of lines of data, yet no computer training was provided. I was one of the few reps who successfully struggled with the databases in Excel, and I was minimally self-taught. But I never thought to look outside the company to learn the skills that would have made my life easier. When you work for a company, you expect them to train you on what they consider important, so this lack of training was overlooked. Fortunately, today a number of progressive companies are offering free tech training for their employees.

At Airbnb, employees can enroll in their Data University to "make their entire workforce more data literate." (Lorenz, 2018) .

Google has just launched Grow With Google (https://grow.google/) to provide a host of free tech training tools and programs for individuals, businesses, schools and startups to help train Americans for tech jobs in the future.

Microsoft partnered with Harvard University's edX.org to offer a professional tech degree to train workers on in-demand data science skills.

Lots of free options are available today to help you increase your technology skills, so make a commitment to yourself to spend at least half an hour a day learning something new about technology in your industry and workplace.

Here are ways to up your tech skills as painlessly and inexpensively as possible:

See What is Available From HR

Go to your HR department and find out what they have available. Do they sponsor any classes? Do they pay for outside training? Will they reimburse you for classes you take outside? They may direct you to an online training platform they subscribe to, or provide self-training CDs or books. It's a start.

Start a Tech Mentoring Group in Your Office

You are not the only person in your company who may be struggling with computer technology. Ask others to form a self-help group, sharing knowledge and resources. Perhaps you can meet in a conference room once a week over a bag lunch. There is generally a tech whiz kid in each office; ask yours to come and mentor or train your group. You can also ask your IT department or support person to send someone to the weekly working lunches. If nothing else, have each person volunteer to research a topic that challenges them, and present what they learned at the next meeting. Or choose a series of YouTube videos to jointly watch at the meetings and discuss afterwards.

Enroll in Non-Credit Adult Education Programs

Many school districts or communities offer low-cost adult or continuing education classes on weekends and evenings. My local school district offers 22 different technology classes at all levels for fees ranging between $55 and $85 per class. In my experience, these classes are taught by working professionals and are very pragmatic and useful. New classes are offered quarterly, so you can pick up multiple skills just one night a week. Plus think of all the nice people you will meet to expand your network!

Take Classes at Your Local Community College

Virtually every Community College teaches technology courses and night or weekend classes are often available. Tuition is very reasonable, and you may end up paying just a couple of hundred dollars for a course.

Depending on your income, you may even qualify for full or partial scholarships through FAFSA or the school's scholarship programs — they generally aren't allowed to discriminate based on age.

A number of community colleges and state universities offer free or reduced tuition for "senior citizens." My local community college district allows any person over a certain age to attend for free if the class is not full by the first day of class. Of course no one promotes these special rates, and many school officials don't even know about these loopholes, so you may want to research them in your market.

Get Free Training From Your Local Unemployment or Job Service Agency

Your local Jobs Services or Unemployment office has tens of millions of dollars of funding for retraining programs, so if you are currently out of work, or you are underemployed, check what free training you are eligible to receive. They may even pay for a training program to certify you for a new well-paying career. The home health aide who comes to bathe and care for my mom had her entire training to become a CNA (Certified Nursing Assistant) paid for by the local job service organization. Likewise, I discovered that a regional tech school will enroll a student and accept a discounted payment from Jobs Services as full payment for a course to train an employee for new career skills. Visit your local Job Services office, meet with a counselor, and learn the myriad of opportunities they offer.

Watch YouTube Training Videos

Everything is available on YouTube, including hundreds of videos about all aspects of computer technology. Just visit *YouTube.com*, enter the word Technology, and see what pops up. Check out some of these companies featured in a YouTube post: *TutorialWebsite.com, TutorialsPoint.com, W3Schools.com*, and *ASP.net*. Watch a number of videos to see what host, topic or style you like, then click on that channel where you will probably find dozens more training videos.

Take Low Cost Online Classes on Udemy or Linda

Udemy.com offers more than 65,000 instructor-led online courses for a modest fee, many providing completion certificates They periodically discount some or all of their courses to just $15, so keep an eye out for special discounts. *Lynda.com* is LinkedIn's version of Udemy, and offers a membership for thousands of different classes.

Listen to Kim Komando, America's Digital Goddess

Kim Komando has been educating Americans about technology for more than 2 decades. *The Kim Komando Show* airs live for 3 hours each Saturday morning. It is carried on over 450 radio stations with an estimated reach of 6.5 million listeners.

"It's not about techies and computer-troubleshooting anymore," the Digital Diva® says. "It's now about a lifestyle — the lifestyle of a digital age." Tune in, listen, and absorb information, jargon, trends, and key words that will be catchy or useful. Set your timer to remind yourself to tune into Kim wherever you are on Saturday mornings. All her shows are available online on demand as well, if Saturdays don't work for you. Find out more at *www.komando.com*.

Join Local Meet Up Groups

Go to *www.MeetUp.com* for your city or community, and search for activities around technology fields. There may be 1,000 or more groups in a 20-mile radius of where you live, and certainly several relating to technology. Programs are generally free or very low cost. You should be able to find programs teaching or cross-mentoring in social media, website programming, blogging, specific programs like WordPress, and much more.

Take Free Classes at the Apple or Microsoft Stores

Both Apple and Microsoft offer free training in their stores, so check out their schedule which should be available online and in the store. These classes are fast-paced, well-structured, and free. What's not to love about learning technology at a tech store?

Subscribe to a Tech Magazine

Subscribe to — and READ — a monthly technology magazine like *PC World*, *Wired*, *Technology Review*, *Popular Mechanics*, *Computer Power User*, *Science News*, or any of dozens of other titles.

Attend Your Local Professional Association Meetings

Your local chapter of your professional association has a Program Committee that searches out vetted speakers who bring new information and insight. Often these will address or touch on technology in your industry, so plan to attend luncheons and special events to learn technology trends while holding a glass of wine or enjoying a nice luncheon — not so bad.

7

EMBRACE LIFE-LONG LEARNING TO UP YOUR SKILLS

Your job and industry are changing daily, and you need to be continually learning new skills in addition to computer technology. It's easier than you think to stay relevant and earn promotions. It's a mindset rather than a skill set. All the resources that we discussed in the prior section are available, and there are many additional resources to explore:

Take Advantage of Tuition Reimbursement Programs

Many large companies offer the opportunity to continue your education for a degree or certification, with the company footing the bill. They may offer to reimburse your college or program tuition up to an amount of perhaps $5,000 per year, as long as you maintain a passing grade of C or better, or a certain GPA.

You can generally take one to three courses per semester at a local in-state college or online university. If you span the course of study over several years, perhaps starting fall semester of Year 1, studying for two years, two semesters per year, and finishing with spring semester of Year 4, you may be able to earn a bachelor's or master's degree with your company funding $20,000 of the tuition. You will probably be required to maintain a passing grade of C or better, and you may be required pay back part of the tuition if you leave before a certain vesting period of perhaps two years. Even so, it's a great way to advance your career tuition-free without giving up your full-time job.

My son Alex started to work for a recognized consulting company as an intern at the end of his junior year, and segued into a full-time position after graduating with his BA in Business Administration from a local university. He thought longingly about quitting his job and going back to school full time to earn his MBA from a prestigious ivy league school. He was looking at $200,000 tuition, in addition to giving up his lucrative job for two years, but it just didn't make sense financially. When his wife Rachel embarked on a two-year master's degree to become a Speech Therapist, which required her to work or study two nights a week, it became clear that a good investment of his time and effort was to continue at his current job, where he was rising in the ranks to Senior Consultant, and simultaneously start taking night classes at his local alma mater. The company paid most of the tuition, and he and his wife both graduated the same week with master's degrees, ready to embark on the next level of their careers.

While an MBA from a top-tier school would have certainly been beneficial, he may never have repaid the nearly $400,000 his full-time studies would have cost, which includes the loss of the two years of salary, job seniority and promotions he earned during that time. Today he is very well employed as a Product Manager for a high-tech division of a leading retailer, earning much more money than I do.

With the right company, you may not even need to reimburse the tuition. Starbucks is offering all its employees — both full time and part time (20+ hours per week) — a chance to earn college degrees at no cost through Arizona State University's online program. Check out the details at the Starbucks' website at *www.starbucks.com/careers/college-plan*. What a great reason to work for Starbucks!

Get a Certification Paid for By the Company

You may not need to pursue a degree program for a long period to up your skills and marketability. You can get a certification or "badge" in a key area of expertise by taking a few classes and studying for an exam. With a couple of advanced certifications added to your credentials, you can readily shift functions if a RIF or division realignment hits your department. You will also be a much more attractive candidate to a potential employer as well. Importantly, this signals to both your current and prospective employer that you are maintaining and growing your skill set to stay relevant.

Apply to Your Company for Full Time Advanced Training

Many companies will fully sponsor rising stars for an executive training program within your field or career trajectory. A number of top schools have 6-month or 1-year residential or online Executive MBA programs which are paid for by the employer, in addition to continuing to pay full salary, housing and all schooling expenses. I know several people who were selected for such programs as part of their grooming for advancement to senior level positions in the company.

All it takes is for you to ask! This signals to your management that you are actively looking to continue your education and learn the skills needed to grow into a key leadership role. The worst they can say in "no", and the best is "yes". Even a "maybe, not now" is not so bad if it puts you on the radar of top management as a potential mover and shaker, regardless of your age.

Make a point of letting your employer know that you plan to work for at least another 10 — 15 years, so they can expect to earn a good return on their investment.

Get Trained in a New Career by Your Local or State Workforce Development Organization

I was amazed to learn that your local Workforce Development or Jobs Services office may pay for training to learn a new career or skill. They invest millions each year to equip unemployed job seekers to find a new valuable career. Their focus is on training for jobs that pay "sustainable wages" of $20 or $25 an hour. Most unemployed older workers only think of Job Services in relation to collecting unemployment benefits, or accessing their job search database, but this is a wonderful option to help you recycle into a great new career. They have partnerships with career study programs that provide them a substantial discount if they pay for your education.

For example, I discovered that Heavy Equipment Colleges of America (*heavyequipmentcollege.com*) charges $10,000 for a comprehensive three week residential hands-on training program to become a heavy equipment operator of a backhoe, wheel loader, crane, front-end loader or other piece of construction equipment at one of their 8 campuses around the country. Another school, The American Crane School (*CraneTrainingTexas.com*) operates a 3-day program for $1,795, which will teach you to operate both telescoping fixed and swing cranes. Most of these pieces of equipment allow you to work inside an enclosed climate-controlled cab so you are not sweltering during the summer or freezing in the winter. They train you to pass the ADEPT (Adaptable Equipment Proficiency Testing) Exam or the National Crane Certification Organization (NCOO) Exam that will allow you to work for more than 1,500 companies with high demand for earthmoving equipment operators — with starting salaries of $25 per hour. The average salary for one of these workers is in the $60,000–$70,000 range annually, according to *Salary.com*. Sounds like a pretty good return on investment, doesn't it? Even more so, since your local Jobs Services organization may negotiate a discounted tuition so you can attend for free if you are unemployed and open to retraining. There are a number of similar schools nationwide, which will train you in many different careers and industries, so do a search for the options near you, and check with your Job Services organization to see if they will help pay the tuition.

Get Job Training Services from Area Non-Profit Organizations

Goodwill Industries, AARP, Dress For Success and literally hundreds of other local and national non-profit organizations provide job training at no or low cost to job seekers of all ages as part of their community outreach activities. Check them out in your area!

Earn Certificates Through Your Professional or Trade Association

Many industry associations offer reasonably-priced training programs and certification exams as part of their professional development programs for members. For example, the American Marketing Association offers the opportunity to earn three different PCM® (Professional Certified Marketer®) certifications, each for a $99 exam fee for members and up to $299 for non-members. You earn a downloadable certificate, and digital badges you can add to your LinkedIn profile. Each certification requires 10 CEUs per year to maintain, which can be earned by online courses like LinkedIn Learning, Lynda, Cousera, MediaBistro, etc. Many different professional associations have similar industry certifications available. Ask your employer to pay for the course and certificate; the worst they can say is "no", and you might save several hundred dollars if they agree.

Pay for Your Own Advanced Training or Certification

Smaller companies may not offer a tuition reimbursement program. But you can still get certified in a valuable career skill on your own at an affordable cost. See what certifications are offered by your local community college — whether or not you already have a degree. They can include jobs like HVAC technician, cosmetologist, teacher certification for working professionals, nurse or nurse's aide, website programmer, paralegal, graphic and web designer, and more. Other available fields include IT, construction and trades, hospitality, education, health and fitness, law enforcement, and much more.

KAllince.com allows you to take as many online classes as you want for $199 for any 12-month period. Our local job services organization provides a free subscription to any qualified student enrolled in their program; check to see if yours does.

Check out *Ed2Go.com*, sponsored by local colleges or universities. It offers hundreds of different work-at-your-own-speed online classes, many leading to certifications, with each class costing between $99 and $199.

Career Builder offers *RightSkill.com*, in conjunction with Capella Learning, "to help workers up-skill and re-skill for in-demand jobs." (Lorenz, 2018).

Many other online programs are available; check with your local community college to find out which ones they support.

And don't forget *Udemy.com*. Many of their thousands of classes lead to valuable certifications. My son Alex and my "adopted" son Ryan are both studying programming online to augment their college degrees. It makes them more employable, more valuable and relevant to the teams they are leading or working with, while providing them with fallback skills in case of an unexpected job loss. All this can be achieved for a couple of hundreds of dollars and working on your own time at your own speed. Udemy has even offered several site-wide sales, where you can buy any class for just $15, providing hundreds of dollars of savings for some high-tech classes. Register to get alerts about sales which may make this a must-pursue option.

According to George Hempe, CEO of Workforce Solutions Alamo, "Today, employers are much more concerned with certifications and demonstrated competency rather than degrees. They want employees with certified skills who can become productive immediately. Nothing provides that guarantee better than certifications in the relevant skills required by the job."

Finish That College Degree That You Started Years Ago

More than 5 million Americans started but never finished their college degrees. They are discouraged by many colleges and schools which no longer recognize or accept prior credits, and expect you to start all over again to get a degree, regardless of your current skills and expertise.

I employed an accountant who was just one class away from finishing her bachelor's degree when her soldier husband got transferred overseas, and newly-pregnant, she accompanied him to his new assignment. She planned to finish her degree during the summer, but needless to say, life got in the way. Seventeen years later, she had to restart her degree program as a freshman, with no recognition for the courses she had taken or her decades of accounting experience with companies that didn't require the degree. Without a degree, she couldn't sit for her CPA exam, and was stuck as a mid-level staff accountant. So in her 40s she was back in school as a freshman, bored silly and resentful of an academic system that didn't recognize her skills and knowledge.

There is a movement to recognize working professionals for the skills they have learned and earned and to fast-track them to finish their degrees quickly and as painlessly as possible. According to a 2015 article from NPR ED, dozens of competency-based degrees are available from a range of traditional non-profit and for-profit universities, as well as more than 10 universities which are exclusively competency-based. NPR reported that more than 140,000 undergrads and 57,000 graduate students were pursuing competency-based degrees where they can demonstrate their expertise either through standardized testing, submission of work history, project submissions documenting their expertise, or a combination of the three.

I met Dr. Chrissann Merriman, Interim Director of Distance Learning, of The University of Mary Harding-Baylor (www.umhb.edu) who stated, "This is the trend of the future. Our country needs to help these five million underemployed workers complete their degrees quickly and affordably, to contribute to the workforce which is demanding the skills they bring to the table." If you have given up, now is the time to rethink the difference a college degree will make to your employability and your self-confidence, and explore this option.

8

LOOK AS YOUNG AS YOU CAN WITHOUT LOOKING SILLY

While the above strategies help you make substantive increases in your skill level, changing the way you look subtly changes perception of you as a person who will fit into the team. You want to be perceived by younger workers as a mature colleague, but not remind them of their mom or dad, or heaven forbid, a grandparent.

Regardless of your age, now is the time for a head-to-toe makeover to erase decades from your appearance.

This is not about beauty and vanity; rather it's about perception and increasing your hireability. The goal is to look like you're 40 or 45, not like you're 20 or 25. But you will also benefit from feeling younger and more vital when you look younger.

Think of yourself as a fine bottle of wine. Without even noticing, your bottle has accrued a layer of dust. Your label has become faded and perhaps scuffed or scratched over the years. The price sign on the shelf is yellowed or gone all together.

If you want to have that fine bottle of premium aged vintage sold at top dollar, it needs to be dusted off, wiped clean of the years of neglect, and repositioned on the top shelf. That's what a makeover will do for your career.

This was really hard for me. I was telling my longtime friend and business partner John about writing this book, and when I mentioned this chapter, he said, "You need a makeover too. Your hair is out of date." I was shocked. I curtly replied, "No it's not. I love my hair like this. I've worn it this way for 20 years." I was stunned to realize that I had not even noticed my look aging from stylish to dated.

I ran into a retired colleague about my age at a recent Ted Talks, and I thought she looked wonderful and so much younger with a sleek short bob in an asymmetrical cut. She raved about Elva, her stylist, and gave me her phone number.

When I finally got the nerve to go to see Elva, I wanted a new hairdo that was not fundamentally different from what I was familiar with — just younger and more stylish. Basically, I didn't really want to change.

I showed up to the salon with freshly washed hair in natural ringlets and showed her prior photos that I liked. She asked me how I fixed my hair, and I explained how I blew dry my hair with a straightening brush on a hair dryer, then used a large curling dryer to add some more fullness. She grabbed my ringlets and announced, "You have naturally curly hair; you are going curly from now on." I was stunned. I had never even considered curly hair as an option; I had always worn straight hair that I considered to be sleek and professional. With great trepidation, Elva cut and styled my hair into a wildly curly mass — and it looked fabulous!

At first, I wasn't convinced, but I got rave reviews from everyone, who said, "I love your new hair style; it makes you look 10 years younger." That sold me on it!

After playing with it for several weeks to get a consistent curly look, I now fix my hair in just about a minute, applying styling mousse and then "scrunching" the hair up all over my head to let it dry in ringlets. When completely dry, I brush it out, scrunch it some more, and then spray the curly mass with a soft sticky spray and I'm ready to head out the door.

The purpose of this story is to acknowledge that change is scary but can have great results even when we least expect it. Let your imagination run wild and re-invent the way you look!

It All Starts with the Hair

The easiest and fastest way to roll back the clock is changing your hair's color, cut, and style. Go to a different stylist or barber, even if you love your current stylist. She sees you through familiar eyes, just like you see yourself. Instead, go to a stranger who has no perception of what you should or shouldn't look like.

Color is very personal, and some people look fabulous with pure silver or salt and pepper hair. My friend Sue has had beautiful silvery-white hair for as long as I have known her, more than 15 years, and she looks great. But generally, gray or graying hair makes you look much older. If yours gets a yellow tint, it makes you really look old. Ask your stylist for advice, spend time looking through style books, and try something new and different.

I'm not a stylist, but as a career coach, my general advice is to restore your original hair color if possible, and cover up the gray or white. Color washes out over time, and your hair may become pale, muted, or dull. Ask your stylist about highlights or lowlights so your color looks more natural. What looks bad on everyone is grown out roots of any color. So you need to conscientiously maintain your color every four to six weeks. And this advice is not just for women; men need to do the same.

Professional coloring can be expensive. Let your stylist perfect the color the first time, then learn how to apply your own color at home using either a packaged kit or mixing toner with color to get the right hue. Ask your stylist for the color and brand that she used on your hair. Then go to a beauty supply store like Sally's and show them your beautiful newly-colored hair and ask to match it. A good colorist will send you home with everything you need to maintain your color at home.

Do what I did and go bravely into the unknown with a talented and recommended stylist. Everything depends on the cut, so be willing to pay top dollar for a stylish cut created by a talented stylist.

It is generally a bad idea for anyone with dark hair to go very blonde, or for people with light or white hair to go dark. Roots grow out fast, eyebrows don't match, and your hair color may not go well with your skin color.

On the other hand, I know some women who look fabulous in dark red hair. So ask your stylist for recommendations, then go and try out your new look.

It will take time to get your style to work for you, but with practice you will make your hair look almost as good as the stylist does. To replicate the style at home or with your next stylist, take lots of photos from all sides.

Men, the same thing goes for you. You may want to abandon your shaggy cut, or leave a military buzz cut and white "sidewalls" to new recruits. Get a stylish cut and professional color. Leaving a bit of gray at the temples may make you look distinguished; try it out, then ask several women how they think it looks.

If you are balding, you can live with it, or shave your head like Yul Brenner in "The King and I." Shaved heads are considered cool and masculine by a number of women today. But a comb over is never a good option.

With advances in hair transplantation over the past years, you might be able to regain a good head of hair with companies like Bosley or Hair Club For Men (*www.hairclub.com*). They are expensive, but will definitely help you look years younger and more vital. Expect to pay between $5,000 and $12,000 or more depending on how much hair needs to be transplanted.

Men, nothing makes you look older than white or gray facial hair. Young men have been dying to grow a beard or mustache since they were in high school, because it makes them look older. It also makes YOU look older. You can look 10 — 15 years younger just by shaving off all your facial hair, especially if it is white or gray.

It may be scary and disconcerting, and many people won't recognize you. But this is a time of reinvention, and you can strip decades off your look in just the few minutes it takes to shave your beard or mustache. And if you absolutely hate it, you can always let it grow back in just a couple of weeks.

And if you absolutely can't part with the facial hair, consider having it professionally colored.

Lose The Glasses

The next easiest fix is to get rid of your glasses. Women have been taking off their glasses for photos forever; now is the time for both men and women to keep them off for good.

Today you can get contact lenses with prescription lenses that act just like glasses, so ask your eye doctor to help you find the right prescription and brand of contacts. He may even provide samples to try out. Today you have the option to get soft lenses and extended-wear lenses that make it easier to manage and less irritating on the eyes. Order your contacts online or get them from your eye doctor.

When you reach Medicare age on your 65th birthday, you will be eligible for cataract surgery to replace cloudy lenses with new clear lenses. Most of us at that age do have cataracts to some degree. Ask your ophthalmologist if you qualify through Medicare or your private insurance. While you generally have the surgery in an outpatient clinic, it is quick and painless, with just a day to recuperate at best.

Medicare will replace your damaged lenses with new clear lenses, but they won't pay for the specialized prescription lenses. While the surgery is free (less deductibles and co-pays), you will end up paying around $5,000 for a pair of prescription implant lenses that will allow you to live glasses-free for the rest of your life (hopefully).

I got Symphony multi-focal lenses, and I ended up with one eye focused for distance and the other for reading, so when the two focus together, I get good visibility for both applications, and can't tell the difference from my more youthful pre-glasses vision of 20 years ago.

Cataract surgery is generally done in an ambulatory medical clinic or hospital, while follow-up adjustments are done in the doctor's office. It took me a couple of office visits for the eye doctor to "tweak" the settings to get the right vision, but these are generally free and included in the original surgery price.

Without the multi-focal lenses, your vision will be clearer, things may look brighter, but you will still need reading or driving glasses to adjust your vision, just like you did before the surgery. You must make your choice before the surgery, as it can't be changed once the surgery is over.

Most doctors offer credit programs from Care Credit (*www.carecredit.com*), which provides 12-month interest-free payment terms. But be careful — if you don't pay off the full balance by the end of the 12-month term, they may charge you a high rate of interest calculated over the original value of the loan. $5,000 is a lot, but may be worth it if it helps you look younger and keep your job longer. It will also save you from buying glasses every year going forward. It was worth it to me to live glasses-free for the rest of my life.

Update Your Makeup

Another quick fix to look younger fast is to update your makeup, ladies. Lipstick colors change, eyebrow styles shift, trends come and go, and you may need to transition to a cosmetics line that provides more coverage, or a different type of translucency.

Makeup manufacturers often provide makeovers as part of their sales and marketing programs. Get a makeover, because you will want to be re-educated on new makeup trends and find a new look that suits you at this age.

I personally have used Mary Kay makeup for the last 30 years and love it. Mary Kay reps are everywhere. If you don't have a friend who is a distributor, post on Facebook that you are looking for a consultant who is recommended by someone you know, and you will certainly get a referral quickly. As a last effort, visit *MaryKay.com*, click on Find an Independent Beauty Consultant, and enter your zip code for a list of consultants nearby.

Mary Kay consultants are not allowed to touch your face; instead, they will provide you with many different samples and demonstrate and coach you on how to apply the different beauty products to your own face. Listen to the advice you receive! Applying makeup is such a routine activity that you will unconsciously do it the same way you have always done it. Break old habits so you can adopt new ones! Make sure you write down the steps, and what colors and products you use, and how to apply them. Take lots of pictures in full sun and artificial light. The subtle change in updating your make up, coupled with a new hairstyle, can take a number of years off your look and will make you feel younger and more vibrant.

Make Your Smile Great Again

Another quick and fairly inexpensive improvement in your appearance is a brighter whiter smile. A quick option is to get laser teeth whitening treatments at a local dentist or medical spa. I received a series of five treatments at a med spa for $200, and the difference was noticeable after just the first 20-minute treatment. By the end of the five treatments, my teeth were brilliantly white!

A technician inserts gel into soft plastic dental trays, which are placed in your mouth and around the teeth. A contraption stretches your lips open, so a brilliant laser light which is focused on the trays bleaches the enamel of your teeth. You may lay back in a massaging lounge chair with wonderful massage and soothing music distracting you to a degree from the bright light and semi-open mouth, and the occasional drool that escapes. I didn't learn until after my first treatment that they will extend the treatment by 10 minutes for an additional $10. So ask for all their pricing options and packages before you commit.

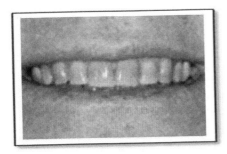 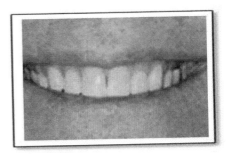

The expression "long in the teeth" refers to an older person. Of course your teeth don't get longer as you age; instead your gums withdraw to show the roots of the teeth unless you carefully maintain dental health with frequent cleanings and dental work. Missing, crooked, stained, or damaged teeth will distract from your appearance and can make you look much older. And coffee-stained teeth look old and unsightly on everyone!

This may be the time to discuss options with your dentist. If you have teeth missing, you might consider crowns, bridges, or dental implants. White porcelain crowns look more natural than silver or even gold crowns or dental work.

If you have severe gum disease, or severely damaged or brittle teeth, you may choose to remove all your teeth and get dentures.

Full dentures vary greatly in price and quality, but online research indicates a price range of $2,500 to $8,000 for a full set of removeable dentures. Your dentist may also charge you to extract the teeth, and you will need to clean and repair the dentures periodically.

Removal of all the teeth frequently results in bone loss, meaning your gum shape will change over time, and you may need to buy new sets of dentures periodically. And it may take several days or even weeks after pulling all your teeth before you are able to wear even temporary dentures while the gums heal.

My dad had full dentures for years, and he hated them. They never fit right, his bite was off, they slipped around in his mouth, and food got caught under them when eating. It was a daily battle, and he regretted his decision to have all his teeth pulled and replaced with a full set of false teeth.

The good news it that today, you can opt for dental implants for a more natural look and feel, and a permanent solution to tooth loss. You can replace one tooth, multiple teeth, or the entire upper or lower set of teeth.

The process is fairly simple. The damaged teeth are extracted in one day, and anchoring screws are inserted into the bone of the jaw, which in turn are used to attach temporary crowns, so you leave the office with attractive functioning teeth in place. When the healing process is complete and the gums have stabilized, which takes about six to eight months, the temporary crowns are removed and replaced with carefully-crafted custom teeth made of durable zirconia material.

ClearChoice Dental Implant Centers provide comprehensive dental transformation through a growing network of more than 43 locations throughout the country. Throughout the ClearChoice network, their teams of experts have performed over 40,000 dental implant treatments all over the country. Each office is equipped with a full dental lab, where the implants are custom made to your specifications.

Treatment plans vary based on each patient's needs, and you can attend a free consultation with a ClearChoice network doctor, who will evaluate each patient and provide an exact cost. Third-party financing options are also available.

Online comments indicate that a single tooth implant can cost between $2,000 and $4,000, with a full mouth of implants costing up $30,000 or $40,000. While this is a substantial investment, it is a lifelong solution to restoring your teeth and replicating a natural eating experience, and one which you might want to explore. Find out more at *ClearChoice.com*.

For other dental work, consider contracting with Careington Dental Plan (www.*careingtondental.com*) if you are willing to work with a dentist who belongs to their network of providers. A friend had $8,000 of crowns done for less than $2,000 at a Careington dentist. A personal membership costs just $8.95 per month or $89 per year, while a family plan costs $16.95 a month or $169 per year. It can save you thousands if you anticipate a lot of dental work — which most of us baby boomers unfortunately need.

The bones of our jaws shrink with age, and your teeth may become crowded or overlap with time. See an orthodontist to find out how to straighten them. Most older professionals will shy away from metal braces, preferring invisible Invisilign braces (www.*invisalign.com*). These new generation "invisible" braces cost between $3,000 to $9,000 in the US. The company claims they will straighten teeth up to 50% faster than traditional metal braces when you get weekly adjustments. You may be able to get some insurance reimbursement for the braces, and they qualify for pre-tax funding from your FSA account. Again, you can fund the difference with Care Credit.

Smile Direct Club (*www.SmileDirectClub.com*) offers a brilliant way to straighten and bleach your teeth at the same time, and is a much less expensive do-it-yourself-at-home option. It costs less than half of traditional braces — just a one-time fee of $1,850, or $250 down and $80 per month. You get a 3-D scan in their office, or take impressions at home, which are then used to create the clear plastic retainers that you wear all the time except for eating or drinking. You receive a one-time shipment of a whole series of retainers for both your upper and lower teeth that, week by week, will result in a gradual shifting of the teeth to the desired position. The treatment includes a whitening process, and generally takes about six months to complete. For $99 you can buy a maintenance retainer to keep your teeth from shifting position again. This appears to be a much lower-cost option and has received great online reviews from hundreds of satisfied customers. I went to a local Smile Club office to investigate the program and was so impressed that I signed up!

Get Rid of the Bags Under Your Eyes

Somehow over the past few years, my eyes developed huge bags which I only noticed when I stopped wearing glasses. Where in the world did they come from? I tried lots of different beauty creams, watched YouTube videos of young girls who thought they had bags, and wasted a lot of money on products that don't work. I saw advertising that drove me to my local drug store, but could never find an employee who knew enough about cosmetics to help me find the right product.

I finally tried Jeunesse® Instantly Ageless™ wrinkle cream (*www.instantlyagelessofficial.com*), from Facebook ads showing huge bags disappearing in just three minutes. It works surprisingly well and lasts for most of the day. It comes with a subscription plan which auto ships every couple of months. The product appears to be made of silicate (a type of clay) and visibly tightens the skin while it dries. You can actually feel it working! It cakes and peels if you apply it too thickly, and loses effectiveness if it gets wet or you use moist or oily makeup on top of it. But all in all, it's a lot better than seeing huge bags every time I look in the mirror. Similar products are offered by Plexiderm and some traditional cosmetics companies.

You can also have bags removed surgically, in a process called a lower eyelid bleth (blepharoplasty) This is cosmetic eye-lid surgery performed by a plastic surgeon who removes excess skin from under the lower eyelashes. Fine scars are rarely seen and can be covered by eye makeup. In less severe cases, the surgeon can remove a pouch of fat from under the lower lid as a less invasive (and less expensive) option. This will not remove dark pigmentation or discoloration but does result in smother tighter skin under the eyes.

The lower eyelid lift is a purely cosmetic surgery, so Medicare insurance won't pay for it. It will cost around $5,000 for both lower eyelids. However, your ophthalmologist may add it to your cataract surgery, saving you money for pre- and post-op care and facility use. You may be able to pay for it using Care Credit to spread payments out over time.

Have an Upper Eyelid Lift — Paid for By Medicare!

If you have heavy baggy upper eyelids which are so droopy that they affect or restrict your vision, you may qualify for an upper eyelid lift or bleth (blepharoplasty) paid for by insurance! This surgical procedure is conducted in an outpatient clinic or hospital, and consists of removing a half-moon shaped piece of skin from the upper eyelids, just above the eyelashes.

For insurance to pay, your eye surgeon will conduct a series of tests, showing your range of vision with your eyelids in normal position, versus having them pulled or taped open for full vision. If you qualify based on vision impairment, Medicare will pay for the surgery (less any deductibles or co-pays). Without insurance reimbursement, you are looking at another $4,500 to $5,500 depending on the surgeon. But it makes a huge difference!

For years my upper eyelids were so droopy it looked like I just was looking out of slits. Whenever photos were being taken, the photographer would say "Open your eyes." My eyes WERE open; they just always looked closed. Now I love my younger, more attractive upper lids, and I can wear mascara which won't get all smudged onto the upper part of the lid like it did in the past. The surgery and recovery were fast and painless, and I was out of sunglasses and back to wearing make up just two weeks after surgery. I do heal quickly, so you may have a slightly longer recovery, but even then, it's well worth it!

   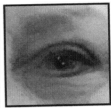

Consider a Full Facelift

Upper and lower lid lifts are a part of a full facelift, which can take a decade or more off your appearance. There are at least two different methods, depending on the invasiveness. Some plastic surgeons will make a long cut above the face and all across the hairline, leaving scars which change the position of your hairline and require bangs in the front to cover the scar. Other less invasive lifts can be performed with a small incision under the chin and around and behind the ears, so you don't have to change your hair style dramatically.

The average cost of facelift cosmetic surgery ranges from $6,000 to $15,000, depending on the extensiveness of the surgery, according to *www.YourPlasticSurgeryGuide.com*. The cost includes anesthesia ($1,000 to $1,300), facility or hospital fee ($500 to $2,000), with the balance for the surgeon's fee. Recovery can take several months, but within 6 months, numbness and scars are generally gone.

I visited a local office of Sono Bello (*www.lipo.sonobello.com*), one of 40 surgical locations across the country. The less invasive facelift which they specialize in will cost around $10,000 to $12,000, and will be done in their local clinic, and not in the hospital. It can include both the upper and lower eyelid lift and tightening of the muscles of the face and under the chin to remove jowls at the jaw line, and the baggy skin and "turkey wattle" under the chin. You wear a bandage wrapped around your head and face for a week, and full recovery can take several weeks or months. If money were not an issue, I would definitely have a face lift today.

Lose Weight (I Would if I Could)

Losing weight can make you look and feel so much younger! Just a few pounds can make a difference. You will:

+ Take pressure off arthritic knees to make walking easier
+ Look younger
+ Appear to have higher energy when you walk
+ Look more youthful

Those of us who always battle with weight know all this, and we would lose weight if we could. However, it is important to discuss weight loss as a veritable fountain of youth because it dramatically impacts your potential for being hired.

With the added incentive of getting or keeping a job, you may want to take steps now to lose 25 pounds — or whatever the magic number is to get and look trimmer.

Go on a Lifestyle Diet You Can Live With For a Long Time

You can join a lifestyle-coaching program like Weight Watchers, or join a weight loss program like Jenny Craig or Nutrisystem which sell prepared food in prepackaged portion sizes. The South Beach Diet (*SouthBeachDiet.com*) and The Paleo Diet (*ThePaleoDiet.com*) both offer hope for many people who have battled their weight in the past and are looking for a low-carb high-protein program that works.

The only thing that has let me lose weight or keep it off over the past 20 years has been the Atkins low-carb diet (*Atkins.com*). When I stay on it, I lose weight or maintain my weight goal; when I go off it I gain weight. Today Atkins offers fabulous low-carb frozen dinners, and wonderful low-carb candies which actually taste great. I can generally adjust any meal to eliminate carbs and replace them with salads, green veggies or more protein. For me, following a low-carb diet has to be a lifelong eating habit, which is not easy. At this point I am not winning the weight battle, but I am working on it, and I am determined to get my body back in shape.

Unfortunately, there are no quick fixes or easy ways out. Try to lose five lbs. this month, and then another five lbs. in another month or two, constantly working towards your goal.

Get Fit and Exercise

As we grow older, our metabolism tends to slow down, and we may need to embrace a fitness program to help in our weight loss or stabilization program. It is a key to looking fit and healthy, and getting rid of unsightly lumps and bumps. Pick a fitness program that works for you; it will make you healthier, happier, stronger, thinner and fitter. Exercise increases energy as well. One expert recommends briskly walking 15 minutes away from the front door and then 15 minutes back, providing the necessary 30 minutes a day of exercise required for a healthy life.

There are dozens of gyms and fitness clubs to choose from, and they all offer new member discounts. Look for special sales in January (diet month) and May (swim suit month), and check to see what deals you can find on Groupon or *LivingSocial.com*.

A personal trainer can help you craft a fitness plan that will work with your lifestyle and physical limitations. You can schedule a one-time consultation, or monthly, weekly or multiple sessions each week. Personal trainers generally average around $50 per 30-minute session; longer sessions can run 60 or 90 minutes, and logically cost more. You can find a personal trainer by referral, or at your local health club.

Consider Body Contouring or Liposuction to Lose Fat Fast

If you simply can't lose unsightly fat accumulated in specific parts of your body, consider help from a plastic surgeon for body contouring. A host of new non-surgical techniques, among them laser or sound frequency programs, melt away the fat. Each procedure at a traditional plastic surgeon costs a minimum of $5,000. So perhaps investing modest amounts for a gym membership, personal trainer, or diet program first would be wise, only considering the more-costly laser programs if you feel other efforts are not working.

I researched body contouring at Sono Bello (*www.Lipo.SonoBello.com*), and got a quote of $12,000 to $17,000 for full body contouring, using liposuction and laser or light contouring. In this minimally-invasive process, the doctor first "liquifies" the "fluffy fat" in the target area with a light or laser, and then inserts a fine cannula or straw in different places and vacuums the fat out. The entire full-body process may take two or three treatments to achieve dramatic transformation, dropping up to two or three pant sizes, from perhaps an 18 to a 14.

They will work on just one stubborn area, or multiple areas, depending on your needs, and will negotiate substantial discounts if you haggle well or express concerns about the cost. You can finance this whole program over 18 months on Care Credit. Recovery is fast, and you can be back to work in just three days after treatment.

Again, if money were not an issue, I would definitely do this.

Get Manicures and Pedicures

As you get older, your nails may become thicker, more brittle, or ridged. Toenails become thick and ingrown, and often dark with fungus. Look into getting pedicures and manicures to keep your hands and feet looking younger and vibrant. Check with your doctor or podiatrist; sometimes insurance plans will pay for monthly pedicures as treatment for ingrown toenails.

Get a Wardrobe Makeover to Dress For Mature Success

One of the fastest ways to look younger is to update your wardrobe for a more contemporary look and one which is flattering to your age and current weight and body shape.

Your closet is almost certainly stuffed to the ceiling with old, outdated, poorly fitting or worn and stained clothing. Be ruthless in changing your wardrobe, and recognize that you can't do it alone.

Invite a friend who cares about you, and who has excellent fashion sense and good taste, and work on this painful task together. Plan to spend at least half a day completely purging your closet of everything that doesn't make you look fabulous. Make sure you have a full-length mirror or two to model in front of with good natural lighting.

Pull everything out of your closet and stack it on your bed, or work section-by-section, and clear out each section of your closet before putting clothing back in. Then decide how you plan to organize your wardrobe:

- By piece — blouses or shirts, pants, jackets, etc.
- By color — group all clothing by color, and arrange colors in a logical sequence like a rainbow, with black and white at opposite ends
- By ensemble — group items you will wear together, and hang them together on the same hanger

✦ By season — summer vs. winter if you have dramatic seasonal differences.

Then try on and inspect each item in your closet. Toss out anything that is torn, worn, faded, dated or shabby. Eliminate any item that just doesn't fit or look right. Discard anything in colors that make you look pale or bilious. Get rid of all those garments that are two sizes too small; perhaps you've been keeping them for years hoping to lose weight to fit into them. When you do lose the weight, you will probably see that they are outdated, and will want something new anyway. Big shoulder pads are out, and so are any garments with them. You will be amazed how many garments are dirty or stained. Wash them if they are washable and say goodbye to anything that is hopelessly stained.

We Americans tend to have way too much clothing, and often buy garments because they are on sale. So you may have separates without the right accessories, or garments that were priced right but just don't work for you. Set them aside today and drop them all off at a local charity thrift shop.

My favorite charity for discarded professional clothing is Dress For Success®, a national charity with local offices throughout the country. They provide a professional suit, shoes, some accessories, along with help with makeup, grooming and coaching to prepare an out-of-work woman so she can present herself professionally for job interviews. When she lands a job, the organization provides additional clothing to help her dress appropriately for her position. The organization also provides help with résumé preparation, job search activities, interview skills and more to help break the cycle of unemployment and poverty. Find our more at www.DressForSuccess.org. Many local branches have a new program for men, called Career Gear, so men's professional clothing is also welcome.

To start your closet rebuilding, select only those garments that make you look and feel fabulous. Model each one to make sure the fit is right, the length is good, the shoulders look natural (big shoulder pads scream '80s), the fabric is wrinkle-free, and it is clean and wearable. Create striking ensembles that portray the professional look you want to establish for your personal brand.

Wardrobe Makeovers for Women

Ladies, start with dresses first, then suits, jackets, and pants. Match each dress to appropriate jackets, shoes and jewelry. Choose several blouses and tops for each suit, and select stunning jewelry and accessories to create a pulled-together look for each top. Coordinate a great look for each key color of suit — slacks or skirt, top, jacket, jewelry, and shoes, and place them in the closet. Look for purses or scarves that fit the look. Make sure hems and sleeves are the right length. If they need to be altered, fix them yourself, or if they are worth spending $10 to fix, take them to a tailor. You might find a reasonably-priced seamstress at a local dry cleaner or at *www.taskrabit.com* or similar site.

Set aside five to ten outfits to wear around the house, to the gym, or on weekends. You really don't need more. Hard as it may be, donate to charity anything that doesn't create a great polished look.

Be ruthless about shoes, too. Try on each pair and walk around in them for half an hour. If they aren't comfortable enough to stand in for an hour, give them away. If they are scuffed, dull, have lost their heel pad, or have heels that are too tall or too short, get rid of them.

Many people have foot challenges as they get older and it is hard to find shoes which are both comfortable and attractive. Women will generally want to choose lower heels. Shop for shoes based on comfort and consider soft rubber soles like nursing shoes. Try gel insoles to make shoes fit better. Check out SAS shoes (*www.sasshoes.com*), available at more than 100 company stores throughout the country, as well as other specialty shoe retailers.

At the end of this closet makeover, you should have maybe 50 to 60 total garments in your closet, which you can mix and match to create at least 40 different looks — enough for a two-month period, five days a week. After you have arranged them by color or ensemble, check for any wardrobe voids to fill in with new contemporary outfits.

Select five or six fabulous ensembles for special occasions — cocktail dresses, evening gowns, casual or cruise wear, etc. Keep one beautiful short coat, another dress-length coat, and a rain coat.

Remember, keep no more than five to ten at-home outfits; you can only wear one at a time. Toss out old separates that don't fit into a good-looking outfit. You will end up always picking out those one or two blouses or tops that look the best anyway; the rest will just take up space in your closet.

If you are rigorous, you will probably discard half to two-thirds of your wardrobe!

Then reward yourself and go shopping to fill any wardrobe voids. A couple of new blouses in contemporary colors and styles, a new suit or two, and new comfortable shoes can give your wardrobe a much needed and welcome facelift.

I believe every woman deserves to own a gorgeous red suit! Be bold, go red! Unless your coloring doesn't go with red, you can project a strong statement of confidence and power in a red suit or dress. And you will stand out from the sea of dark suits in any professional gathering.

Depending on your age, weight and figure, you can wear dresses, suit-dresses, or suits with skirts or pants with coordinating blouses and blazers. You may not need to wear the power suit a younger woman might choose; you can probably get away with a softer look, as long as it is professional and elegant and looks good on you. If you are re-entering the workforce or need to strengthen your personal brand to establish your credentials or authority, you might opt for the power suit look.

If you are trim and slender, you have many attractive looks to choose from, and can shop at just about any retailer for great professional attire.

I am past plump, so I battle to look good. The Chicos look works for me. At this point I wear primarily soft microfiber knits in solid colors, like the Chicos Travelers Collection (*Chicos.com*). I recently had photos taken at an event and discovered that contrasting tops and pants looked awful with my more-than-full figure. So I have moved to a monochromatic look — jacket and dress, or jacket, top, and pants, all in one color. I accessorize it with bright fairly large jewelry or scarves which add color and a focus around my face. Dress and jacket sets in black, navy, royal blue, dark teal, purple and red work for me. I wear only black and navy-blue pant sets, with more than a dozen necklaces and scarves to add bright splashes of color. At least two or three sets of jewelry or bright scarves go with each basic suit, and that's all the variety I need to look as good as possible without looking the same.

I have found a line of Chicos look-alike microfiber knit dresses, pants, jackets and blouses at a fraction of the cost. *JostarUSA.com*, the manufacturer, has a website which displays all their products, but only sells wholesale to stores with resale certificates. I order Jostar brand garments from several different online retailers; Amazon and Ebay both carry the line, and my favorite mail order store is *AFashionShowBoutique.com*. I buy all the Jostar solid basics, then add Chico accessories for that special flair.

The Chicos look may not be right for you. You need to "find your look" and adjust your wardrobe around your realities today — height, weight, fitness, lifestyle, etc. While it may be different from how you looked just a few years ago, once you refresh your wardrobe with a friend's help, you will look and feel great.

Fashion Makeover for Men

Men, you too can benefit from a fashion makeover, but it's much easier for you than for a woman, in part because you generally have fewer garments. Most professional jobs require a suit as basic attire, even if you take off your jacket, roll up your sleeves and loosen your tie the minute you walk into the office. If a VIP drops in unexpectedly, you can always slip back into your jacket to look the professional you are. You may look and feel less polished and less competent in shirtsleeves.

Suit fashions mostly vary with just lapel width, front pleats (or no pleats), and pant cuffs (or no cuffs). Unless your suit jacket has enormously wide or pencil thin lapels, it will probably look fine if it is clean, pressed, fits well, and is not worn or shabby. If you have gained weight and your jacket pulls when you button it, or bunches up and wrinkles around your waist or biceps, either lose weight or give it to charity. Wearing it will ruin your professional look.

Your fashion staples will be suits in navy, black, charcoal gray, and perhaps a medium or lighter gray. Light-colored suits get dirty fast, so avoid them. You may want one or two suits in subtle plaids or pinstripes but avoid loud patterns or wide stripes that make you look like a mafia don. Also have several sports coats in solids that coordinate with solid dark slacks or a pair of khakis or dark jeans for casual Friday. If you are a mature professional, you probably have most of these already, and if they are expensive bespoke suits, that's even more fabulous — wealthy men will recognize the design and the finishing touches. The challenge is to discard clothing that no longer fits into your mature professional look.

The easiest way to update your work wardrobe is to buy a few new crisp white or pastel shirts and silk ties that coordinate with your good-looking and well-fitting suits. Shirts with small repetitive patterns may also work, but need to be paired with a solid or striped tie to look best. Get help from your menswear salesman to make sure your look is put together.

Shirts should be long sleeved, generally

with button cuffs, instead of cufflinks, and can have either button down or standard collars. Take care to get the sleeve length right. Shirt cuffs should stick out ½ inch below the hem of your jacket sleeve when you stand straight with your hands at your side. Get rid of shirts with sleeves that are too long or too short. And unless you have exceptional circumstances, don't wear short sleeved shirts under a suit or sports coat — ever.

Once you have landed your job, you may want to relax your look, and a great way to do that is to wear a company-branded polo under your sports jacket, with solid slacks or khakis.

Never wear a clip-on tie — that is so old fashioned and puts your look in the lower income tier. Buy fine silk ties and learn to tie a beautiful Windsor or half Windsor knot. Solid colors work with just about everything; patterned ties are much trickier to coordinate but can add a touch of elegance if selected well. Many stores offer shirts paired with a coordinating silk tie. Unless you have a GQ flair for fashion, I would recommend you buy half a dozen new shirt-and-tie combos to update your look. Crisp and clean will say a lot about you!

Your tie should be of moderate width — generally around three inches wide today. Narrow ties are considered edgy and hip for younger men, while the two and a half inch Mad Men tie has a retro look and feel that can be hip if you can pull it off. Wide ties over three and a half inches wide are hopelessly out of style.

Regardless of the width, your tie should just touch the top or middle of your belt buckle when you stand up with your hands at your side. Avoid wearing your tie too short (looks juvenile or nerdy) or too long (looks sloppy). Check the fashion ads to see if tie tacks or bars are in style. If not, just tuck the tail of the tie into the band at the back of the wide part of the tie.

Wear knee-high dark socks in black, navy, or brown to go with your shoes. A trend among young professionals is to wear bright patterned and funky or irreverent socks with your suit. Use your judgment after you have the job and can feel the vibe of your office.

You may want to invest in a pair or two of new leather shoes to update your look. Unless you work on Wall Street, wing tips are hopelessly out of style. Since you only need new contemporary shoes in black and brown, this is not a major investment that will break the bank, but an updated look, top to bottom, will pay off.

You probably need one attractive long winter coat, and also a long light-weight rain coat which can go over your suit.

Updating your look shouldn't cost a fortune; you can probably do all this, including 2 new pairs of shoes, for under $500. I personally love shopping for men's clothing at Burlington (*BurlingtonCoatFactory.com*) which has great de-signer suits and a wide assortment of shirts and ties, for very reasonable prices. My son recommends JC Penny (*JCPenny.com*) for an excellent collection of reasonably-priced professional wear. Saks Off 5th (*www.SaksOff5th.com*) has good prices on excellent men's shirts and ties, especially under their own Saks Fifth Avenue brand, which is very heavily discounted. Macy's (*Macys.com*) also has good men's fashions, and offers discounts which bring prices more in line with other reasonably-priced retailers.

Pick the store that fits your budget, and connect with a sales person who can become your personal shopper. Ask him or her for suggestions, tips, and trends. Build a rapport, and ask for a call when new fashions arrive that will fit your style.

And while you're at it, throw away all your old baggy worn underwear and socks and buy all new ones. It will cost you less than $100, and will make you feel 10 years younger.

Accessories to Top Off Your Look

Attractive accessories will complete your contemporary look. Carry a soft leather attaché case for résumés, references, work portfolio and personal accessories for

the job interview. Ditch that hard molded Samsonite briefcase — it practically screams old fashioned. Carry a nice leather portfolio with note pad and place for your business cards — and to place their cards during the interview. A good quality but not over-the-top ballpoint or gel pen will complete your look. A Cross pen or similar brand is fine. No need to shell out big bucks for a Mont Blanc unless you are interviewing for a top corporate position where your boss will wear a $2,000 designer or bespoke suit. All of these can be found at reasonable prices at your local office supply store.

Ladies, don't carry both your attaché case and purse to the interview; it will make you look cluttered and clumsy. Instead, take your barest essentials and tuck them into a small clutch bag and carry it in your soft-sided attaché case with your portfolio, pen, and interview materials.

As a general rule, I advise job seekers to take notes with pen on the notepad in your briefcase instead of a tablet or iPad. However, for a mature worker, using your iPad or tablet to show your online portfolio will signal you are tech savvy, which is a good thing for a baby boomer. Just make sure you can use it skillfully; no poking around with one finger to type or struggling to find your portfolio page.

Get Off To a Fast Start to Keep Motivated

Start with updating your hair color, cut and style, brighten your smile with teeth bleaching, replace glasses with contact lenses, update your makeup, ladies, shave the gray beard, men, and update your wardrobe by eliminating what doesn't work and adding a few new items. You should be able to accomplish all this within a week or two, and for under $2,000. And you will look and feel a decade younger.

You deserve to look and feel younger, and it will definitely be worth the investment if it helps insulate you from job loss, or lets you advance to the next round of interviews for a new job.

You will feel fabulous, and that will motivate you to start on the harder steps — like losing weight, getting fit, and straightening or replacing your teeth. People will respond positively to these changes in your personal life and they will make a big difference in your professional life. You will fit in subtly with younger workers, and bosses will equate your younger refreshed look with having more energy and vibrancy.

You deserve to feel as fabulous as you will look.

9

ADOPT YOUNGER ACTIONS, HABITS, TOOLS AND PROPS

Now that you look and feel younger, you need to act younger as well. That doesn't mean childishly or frivolously; it means adopting ways to relate to younger workers through subconscious cues found in the way you act, walk, communicate, get news, and adorn your workspace.

Go Mobile

Today's younger generation is completely mobile. To fit in, you need to embrace and adopt mobile technology in just about everything you do.

Use your up-to-date smart phone for everyday tasks, including reading and sending emails, making appointments and checking your calendar, using online banking, and ordering everything from Amazon. Never ever bring a newspaper into the office, or reference looking up anything in "The Yellow Pages." Run a Google search instead. Use mobile banking; going to a physical bank and talking to a teller is obsolete. Manage your calendar online; ditch the Day-Timer® or pocket agenda for dates and notes; it is woefully low tech. Do not take a paperback in your purse; read everything on a Kindle or mobile phone instead.

Don't ever complain in public about computers or bemoan technology, indicating a resistance to adapt. However, you may complain about passwords, multiple email addresses, connectivity issues or app upgrades.

Use text messaging, Facebook Messenger, and Slack to communicate quickly and easily, even if our old fingers have a terrible time trying to manipulate those tiny keys. Use dictation instead; it's faster and easier. Millennials consider emailing old fashioned, and prefer text messaging, which has an open rate more than four times higher. Whichever you use, make sure you always proofread and correct anything you dictate!

And don't refer to it as "typing," today it is called keyboarding.

Adopt Wearable Technology Even If It's Just a Prop

Watches are dead — unless you own a Rolex, Breitling, Patek Philippe, Mont Blanc or other outrageously expensive timepiece which signals conspicuous wealth and membership in the old boys' club. Instead, sport an Apple Watch or a FitBit. Otherwise, check your phone whenever you want to know what time it is.

Use a Bluetooth earpiece to connect to your smart phone, or wear ear buds wired to your phone to quiet noise in busy open floor plans and shared workspaces.

You can choose to own a GoPro camera system, or fly a drone, to be really cool for an "old guy." Post photos or videos on your Facebook page and mention them as your hobby during an interview.

Get a New Slim Laptop and Carry It With You

Desktop computers are generally a thing of the past. While you may use your clunky desktop computer at home, at work you may be forced to use a laptop that you carry with you at all times. Choose a new lightweight thin laptop, which you can buy at Best Buy or Office Depot for around $300. They will load it with your Microsoft Office suite and a virus protection program (both of which you have to buy of course.)

If your laptop is more than a couple of years old, it's probably obsolete, and you may want a new one if you use it for work. The biggest challenge is the time and effort to load new software, install programs you purchased years ago (and probably forgot the passwords long ago), copy over files, fix settings, and set it up the way you want. This may take several days if you have a lot of files and programs. You can get help with set up and file transfer where you buy your new laptop, but it may cost you some money, generally under $99. Plan to spend time setting up the new computer, with logins and passwords, setting up wifi and printers, and more.

I suggest that you purchase Best Buy's Geek Squad Protection Program for 24/7 tech support (*www.geek-squad-tech-support.com*). It costs $200 for one year, or $350 for three years, and covers up to three different devices (like your desktop computer, laptop and tablet.) I opted for the three year program and found it to be a great value and helped me out of many computer messes quickly and easily. With this program, you will receive online help any time of the day or night, where a tech remotely takes control of your computer and runs diagnostic programs to determine what needs fixing, makes any needed changes, removes viruses and malware, and optimizes performance. Or take your computer to any Best Buy for free evaluation and many tech services. If your computer dies, they will download and restore your files for free, although you may have to pay for the remote storage device they store the files on, which you get to keep.

I also recommend using a remote file backup system to preserve all your files in case of a fatal computer crash. Yes, we know we should back up our files, but no one ever does. I use Carbonite, which backs up all the files on my computer (but not the programs themselves.) If your computer crashes, your files are safe and can be easily recovered and restored to your new hard drive or computer. Go to *Carbonite.com* and subscribe to an annual membership starting at $60 per year for one computer, or $260 per year for multiple computers. You can also choose automatic cloud backup with Google, One Drive, iCloud, or other online backup and file sharing program, also for a monthly or annual fee.

Most people use PCs, particularly in a business environment, but if you use an Apple laptop, you will be regarded as much cooler and more tech-savvy by younger peers. Apple computers are easy to use, and have lots of bells and whistles, but they are much more expensive. A new MacBook Pro will start around $1,300 and runs up to $2,500 for a larger and fancier model. A Mac uses a completely different operating system and runs programs that may not be readily compatible with PC users. As a professor, I often get assignments submitted in Pages (Apple's word processing program) or Keynote (Apple's presentation program), and I can't open them on my laptop. Microsoft now makes a version of the Microsoft Suite for Apple computers, which can solve this problem to some degree, although many Apple users prefer the built-in Apple programs. It's a choice you have to make.

I am definitely not super tech-savvy. I can't seem to use the touch pad mouse on my laptop, and have to use a remote keyboard and old-fashioned mouse to type just about anything. I set up what I call a poor man's docking station using a legal-sized plastic file tray turned upside down, which lets me set the laptop 3" above the keyboard. Then I tuck the keyboard underneath the laptop to bring the screen to the right distance for typing. I use a Logitech wireless mouse and keyboard combination with a USB stick that plugs into a single port on the laptop. When I travel, I simply close the laptop, and nestle it inside the tray to protect it in my suitcase or brief-case, with the keyboard and mouse pad resting on top. I have to remember to remove the USB stick, as on several occasions it has become bent and unwork-able when jostled in my briefcase. If that happens, I have to run out to an office supply store to get a

replacement keyboard and mouse set to effectively use the computer. If you can use your laptop well, using the built-in keys and finger-controlled mouse, that is great and definitely cooler than my jerry-rigged docking station; but if not, this might make your computer easier to use.

Adopt Fitness as Part of Your More Youthful Lifestyle

Younger workers tend to go to the gym, and talk about cross training, mixed martial arts and Iron Man competitions. They monitor their BMI and respi-ration on their phone or FitBit. They track miles walked every day and will climb steps rather than take the elevator to get in extra paces to meet their goals. Golf and tennis are not on their radar, but racquetball, soccer, rugby and Ironman competitions are.

Learn to fit into the conversation by referencing lifestyle practices of the younger workforce and eliminating old fashioned words from your vocabulary.

Focus on Walking Briskly and Energetically

One of the key attributes that signals age is how briskly you walk. My long-time friend, Jeremy, is a newly-hired 60-something CEO of a small charter aircraft company. He says he is at least 10 or 20 years older than most em-ployees and feels more like a parent than a boss. He is thin and trim and looks young, but he is still aware of how he acts to eradicate concerns about age. To reinforce the perception of youthfulness, he has taught himself to walk briskly, and often jogs across the huge hangar where the planes are staged.

I have awful knees, with a torn meniscus from10 years ago that caused degenerative osteoarthritis in both knees. I take Aleve to reduce inflammation. It helped a lot for several years, but now my knees are bone-on-bone. Sound familiar? I have recently had success with a regimen of 3 shots of Synvisc, rather than having a knee replacement — which is the next stop. I have to force myself to walk gracefully without a limp. It is easier to just clomp along. I have to constantly watch myself when in professional situations to walk briskly without limping.

As we age, we also need to avoid shuffling our feet by lifting them up, and practice taking long confident steps, instead of short hobbling steps which scream "I'm old!" We also need to keep our heads up, look forward or side to side when walking, instead of looking down at our feet. Practice these youthful walking habits.

Hide or Minimize Physical Limitations or Grandparently Actions

You don't want your coworkers to think of you like their grandparent, or even their parent. You should aspire to be seen as a cool older aunt or uncle at worst.

Keep your arthritis and heartburn medicines hidden at work; go to the restroom to take them if possible, or turn your back away from your co-workers when it's time to take that handful of meds.

Don't talk about your "old peoples" injuries and illnesses. It's okay to mention a torn meniscus, but not arthritis or bad knees. The same goes for a bad hip, or a hip replacement. No one needs to know that you have osteoarthritis or osteoporosis; instead say you injured your hip in a skiing mishap. If your shoulders hurt, mention a fall while playing basketball or a torn ACL.

Don't fiddle with your hearing aids or take them out to replace the batteries in public. Instead, adjust them in the rest room or another quiet place. You may be able to control your nearly invisible Bluetooth-controlled hearing aids on your smart phone. Adjusting the volume manually in public is not an option. Don't talk about them either; let them be your own secret. Do go to a hearing specialist and get tested if people complain that you talk too loudly, you aren't paying attention or don't hear them. Better to have discreet hearing aids than keep asking people to repeat themselves or speak up. (My son and his wife nag me about this constantly!)

Don't complain about bad health, aches and pains, a bad back, flat feel, chronic indigestion, or the cost of medical insurance. Don't mention Medicare of Social Security. Millennials feel they are invincible; any health conditions you talk about that don't affect them will peg you as old. Plus many of them resent having to pay for programs for us that they feel may not be around when they are old — which they can't even conceive of.

Of course, if you are dealing with a severe medical condition, or battling cancer or other serious illness, you can and probably should share that with your co-workers. Leave anything relating to your grandkids at home; no pictures with frames stating "I love grandma" or kindergarten art masterpieces stuck to your peg board. Enjoy all those treasures from your precious grandkids at home and with friends your same age.

We already discussed ways to look younger, which includes bleaching your teeth, fixing a not-so-great smile, and replacing glasses with contact lenses or cataract surgery. Keep those fixes private as well. Apply lotion in private to keep skin moist and fix nails which have become yellowed and brittle due to a fungal infection. Once these subtle shifts in your behavior become seamless and natural, you will better fit into a more youthful workplace.

Use Non-Verbal Messaging To Fit In

Use non-verbal techniques to send subliminal messages to younger colleagues that you fit in. For example, Starbucks is where many younger workers get their morning java.

A Starbucks cup in your office is a subtle sign that you are one of them. Even if you don't want to pay $4 for a cup of coffee, just get a stack of Starbucks cups, or reuse an old Starbucks cup with your coffee. Even better, buy a refillable plastic Starbucks cup or mug that you can use over and over again.

Coffee houses are popular with younger workers, and they may frequent a local roaster for their coffee fix. Be aware of this trend so you can fit in.

Individually-brewed coffee and tea made in a Keurig coffee maker also signals that you are with it.

Your younger colleagues may want to go out to lunch for sushi (raw fish — yuck!) or a vegan meal (tofu?). They may rave about kale and amaranth and other weird veggies or grains. Tough it out if needed.

Be prepared for gender differences you never imagined, and don't even frown, let alone grimace in disgust, if a man talks about his husband, or a woman in the office is six feet tall with an Adam's apple and a deep voice. Today it's called gender fluidity or being transgender, and is often referred to LGBT, and boy oh boy, is it fluid.

Likewise, set aside any long-held prejudices about race or religion — showing anything like that will be the death knell to your career in this politically-charged and socially-correct time in our country.

If there is talk about smoking pot or hooking up on Tinder for sex with a stranger, keep a straight face and don't let negative feelings show through.

Working with much younger colleagues has another benefit: you may find you relate better with your own children or grandchildren.

10

DEVELOP A MORE YOUTHFUL COMMUNICATION STYLE

Many of today's workers are at least one or two generations younger than you are. To fit into this younger dynamic workforce, examine their different behaviors, understand or accept them, and copy or replicate them whenever possible or appropriate. Below are several ways you can easily adopt younger communications habits at work.

Text Instead of Email or Call Whenever Possible

Millennials prefer to text instead of talk on the phone, and even more so than reading emails. Send text messages rather than leaving a voicemail message that will never get heard. In fact, you don't even need to leave a voicemail; most people will see that they missed a call from you and return it before checking messages. Use the dictation feature on your phone rather than trying to type. Always proofread your text before you hit send. Noting the errors made by Siri will help you enunciate more clearly, so that's a hidden benefit.

Learn to Write Short and Sweet, Almost Cryptically

Today's workers cut their teeth on 144-character Twitter messages, and they value brevity over thoroughness. An emoticon is preferred over words. They speak in almost a coded language of brevity and sound bites. This carries over into written documents at work.

One of my biggest challenges has been to change my written communication style. I was trained to write a memo or follow-up document or meeting minutes in great detail so everyone could read it at any time and understand absolutely everything. The problem? They simply won't read it. Their eyes glaze over and they discard or ignore my emails and memos.

I have had to modify my writing style to be much shorter and crisper, and you can too. Use bullets instead of paragraphs. Write short paragraphs with bold underlined headlines to make quick scanning easy. Use short rather than long complex sentences. Add white space between paragraphs so your readers don't feel overwhelmed. Apply bold formatting to key words to help readers extract or identify relevant topics quickly. Only write about the most critical topics; they will contact you if they need more information.

Make Crisp Presentations And Limit Text

Presentations should be similarly terse:

- Use a big graphic and few words.
- A rule of thumb is to use a font that is the age of your audience. So if you are presenting to 30- to 40-year olds, use a 36 or 40 font; if your audience is 60, use a huge font and few words.
- Use bullets whenever possible. Rather than using full sentences or paragraphs, create a bulleted list with short phrases instead.
- Address one topic per slide and create slides that you can talk through in 30 seconds or less.
- Don't read the slides; instead comment about what the information means.
- Make sure your contact information is on the last slide; you'd amazed how many presentations I find in my files where I have no way to contact the writer for more information.

Use Text Messages Whenever Possible

If you have an important message or need to talk to someone right away, send a text message alerting them to check their email. Avoid leaving voicemails; they may not be heard for days, while text messages are instant and permanent.

Consider adopting group messaging programs like Slack. This hot new free app allows for group instant messaging and permits you to contact each group member individually or as a whole group. If you are on a team, board or task force, this is a great way to facilitate communication rather than numerous emails back and forth. A number of other programs do the same thing; be on the lookout for whatever your company or colleagues are using for group communication.

Use Document Sharing

Set up a free Dropbox account for document sharing and retrieval. If you buy any new personal computer, you will probably be forced into using the Microsoft 360 Office Suite, which allows for group collaboration, and stores documents in the cloud. There are a large number of document sharing programs, including free ones on your Google platform linked to your Gmail account.

Use a Contemporary Email Address

Change your legacy email from AOL, Yahoo, People PC, your cable company, or just about any other email program (these signal you are old and not relevant) and use a free Gmail address instead. You can create many different email addresses and segregate them for specific purposes. I have 15 different emails: my main company email, unique emails assigned by each of the universities where I teach, and a personal Gmail address. I have email addresses for my different book series, and for LinkedIn ProFinder leads. I use my legacy AOL email for old friends and have another old AOL email I use for online purchases only so I don't get spammed to buy things on my main emails.

The great thing is that you can set up your smart phone to receive all your emails from all these different accounts right on your phone. You will be able to see all your emails mixed together or choose to read them account by account. I only keep one or two Gmail accounts open on my desktop at any time, and forward any important email to the main account for downloading or printing. In this way you are always in touch and live a digital lifestyle easily.

Eliminate Cursive in the Workplace

Do you like to write long hand? It's a lost skill today; as many millenials were never taught penmanship in school, and don't feel comfortable writing or even reading cursive. Who would have guessed?

It's important that you modify or adapt your communication style to be younger, fresher, more concise, and more relevant. It just takes being attuned to the work environment, listening as younger workers talk among themselves and observing what their habits and preferences are.

Don't Talk About Politics — It's a Lose-Lose Proposition in the Workplace Today

Younger workers traditionally tend to be liberal and vote Democratic, while older workers tend to be conservative and vote Republican, both by a margin of at least two to one.

The recent election was extremely polarizing, exacerbating the divide, pushing both groups into more extreme positions. Today, many people can't talk civilly about politics with a person of the opposite party.

So any discussion of politics at work is a Catch 22. Your best strategy is to just walk away or change the subject. If you can't, say that you don't feel comfortable talking about politics at work. You have lots to lose, and little to gain, if you respond to any political discussion.

Also, avoid any political signage or bumper stickers on your car or in the workplace.

Be Supportive of a Younger Boss

You may find yourself in a challenging position if you end up working for a younger boss, often one with much less experience. You need to navigate very carefully to protect yourself and your position.

To start, I recommend welcoming your new young boss and congratulating her on her new role. Offer to discuss any concerns she may have and discretely acknowledge the age difference. Keep it from becoming the elephant in the room. Express respect for her talents and abilities, offer acceptance and loyalty to her as your supervisor, and let her know that you are eager to learn from her.

If your new boss is coming from the outside, you might want to say something like, *"I'm here to support you in any way I can. You bring a new vision and direction to the company (or department,) and I look forward to both learning from you and supporting you in any way I can. Please know you can call on me to help you navigate the system to implement your new programs and ideas."*

Become The Department Go-To Person to Leverage Your Experience

For maximum job security, position yourself as the go-to person to help your new boss and other younger workers navigate the system, since you have legacy knowledge of the industry and the company that newer employees don't have. Informally offer to mentor newer or younger workers. You can learn from each other in a beneficial exchange of information.

When you share insights about past actions or programs, try not to sound like a disgruntled know-it-all or nay-sayer. Don't say, *"We used to do this or that..."* or *"We tried that and it was a failure."* Instead, when someone suggests a plan of action that was previously tried (and often failed or was discarded), you might say, *"I think our organization has prior experience testing (or evaluating) that idea. Maybe we can revisit that experience in light of today's technology (or market changes, or competitive situation, etc.), to learn if it's relevant today. Why don't I do some research to find out what was done in the past and I can make a brief presentation of that learning at the next meeting."* That emphasizes the value of your experience, while expressing willingness to accept new ideas and seriously evaluate them.

Your job security goal should be to dispel fears that you will be disloyal or stab your new boss in the back out of resentment or fail to be a team player. Strive to become the go-to person in your department that everyone consults when they want to fly a trial balloon about a new idea or proposal, thus leveraging your years of experience and expertise.

BRAND YOURSELF TO SHIFT-PROOF YOUR CAREER

SHIFT happens. Only you can prevent being left behind in the turmoil by having the required job skills for your current or sought-after position.

Everything in your professional life is shifting — or has already shifted: the employment market, the competition, the workplace, how we work, where we work, what we want from work. We have changed in the eyes of our employer over time and your employer may have changed in your eyes as well.

For the most part, these shifts are beyond your control. These shifts are what happens TO you.

The only way to shift-proof your career is to skillfully establish your personal brand in the eyes of current and future employers. It's all up to you. It takes work but is easier that you think.

We'll discuss the five key ways to enhance your personal and professional brand today that will insulate you, as much as possible, from the negative aspects of the shifting job market, leverage what you're currently doing to go to a higher level, and as a result, improve your hireability and job security:

1. Double down on networking
2. Start your own consulting company
3. Build your professional website
4. Update your résumé and LinkedIn profile
5. Master your social media presence

My book *BRAND YOU! To Land Your Dream Job*, and other ebooks in the *BRAND YOU!* series, are filled with detailed information on topics like Social Media, Networking, and Résumés.

I hope you enjoy exploring key personal branding strategies and how to maximize them, finding them as much fun as I do in writing about them.

11

DOUBLE DOWN ON NETWORKING

As a mature worker, networking is your competitive advantage. You have 30 or 40 years more experience and connections than a younger employee has. So learn to take advantage of it.

The Biggest Mistake the Unemployed Professional Makes

Our profession is in many ways our identity — one of the characteristics of our generation. When we lose our job, a part of our heart and soul goes with it. We are wounded, stunned, unsettled, and may even question our worth. The natural reaction is to retreat to our cave or safe place, hunker down and protectively wrap our arms around ourselves and our egos as we suffer in pain and self-doubt.

If this is you, you probably don't know what to say to a former colleague you meet on the street or at an event. You no longer have a business card to offer. When someone asks the inevitable question "What do you do?" you feel uncomfortable and stammer something about looking into new opportunities or just blurt out that you were laid off and are looking for a job. Awkward! You don't have $200 to spare for your annual association membership and hate to pay $35 for a speaker luncheon at a networking event.

As a result, many unemployed professionals make the same mistake. They withdraw from networking when they should be doubling down. In fact, networking should be the number one job search strategy if you are unemployed or looking for a new position.

Networking Is the Solution for Anyone Looking For a Job

George Hempe, CEO of Workforce Solutions Alamo, recently shared these stats:

* As a rule of thumb, it takes one month per each $10,000 of desired salary to successfully find a job

- If you hope to earn $50,000 per year, expect to spend five months looking for a job.
- For a $100,000 job, plan to be job hunting for 10 months.
- However, by effectively leveraging your personal and professional network, you can cut that time down by half.

Half of all jobs are found through networking. The older you are and the higher your desired salary, the more important networking is.

This means you should invest at least half of your time and effort, and preferably more, in networking,

Network Through Your Professional Association

Take advantage of your membership in your professional associations by serving on the board or mentoring younger members. Volunteer to lead a mentoring group or hold weekly webinars for members seeking to develop their skills. Make sure you show up at industry association events early, to meet and greet everyone as they enter and leave. Be the last to leave, lingering to chat with attendees and help out the organizers.

While many association members may be younger than you are, you will run into lots of your peers and former colleagues at meetings as well. They may be impressed with your leadership and mentoring. Invite that old friend or colleague to lunch or coffee and mention your interest in a new opportunity. Want to keep your current job? Invite your boss to the association's meeting and let him see how highly regarded you are by your peers as an industry leader.

Volunteer to Really Connect

Often, when people go to a networking event, they stand in a corner and nobody talks to them; then they think, *"That wasn't fun,"* and they go home without any benefit from the event or the organization. While it is important to attend networking events, the way to really get to know other people is to volunteer. Sign up for a committee or get a seat on the Board. Organizations are always looking for volunteers.

Before I knew all about networking, I occasionally attended American Marketing Association luncheons and never really engaged with anyone. I felt alone and left out and didn't attend regularly. Then one day the president said, *"Hey, I need somebody to handle Public Relations. Can you do PR?"* I said, *"Sure, I can handle PR, I guess."* With that, I joined the Board, became involved, met everybody in the marketing community and showcased my talents to my peers. That one word *"sure"* moved me from the sidelines of the industry to the inner circle.

When you're on a Board or committee, you're on the inside and in the know. You hear all the industry gossip first. You're recognized in the newsletter. You are introduced and stand up at the luncheons. Most importantly, you know everything that's happening in your industry. You will often hear about job openings in your field before they are made public. At a monthly Board meeting, one of your colleagues may say, *"Did you know Mary just took a new job at XYZ Company?"* You just learned her old job is open. You can call Mary to get information on the open job, who to contact, and maybe even a referral to someone at the company if she left in good standing. All this can happen before the company even posts the job opening on *Monster or Career Builder*! With networking, you can get your foot in the door before anyone else even knows about the job opening.

Three Key Volunteer Committees to Advance Your Goals

Volunteering for your professional or industry organization is very important. Three favorite volunteer positions that I strongly recommend if you are looking to network, meet people and hopefully find a new job: Hospitality, Membership and Public Relations.

1. Hospitality Committee

The Hospitality Committee is responsible for making members feel at home, connecting with other people, and ensuring they have a positive experience at the event or with the organization. So when Joanne attends your organization's event for the first time, you get to go over and say, *"Hello, Joanne, I see you're a new member. Welcome. I'm Diane and I work for XYZ Company. What do you do?"* You can ask questions like, *"Is there anyone in particular you'd like* to meet today?" and "*Tell me a bit about your business.*" So now she is talking and you are learning about her.

Then you get to do matchmaking based on the information you just learned by introducing people to each other: "*Joanne, I'd like to introduce you to Robert, who works in your industry. Why don't you sit together and you can discuss the latest trends?*" Joanne is grateful to you, because she is no longer standing around by herself thinking "*Nobody's talking to me.*" Robert is too because you just brought him a potential customer or colleague. They both think you are wonderful, and they both owe you a favor. It's that simple to connect with two new people through your volunteer role. Of course if Joanne is someone you want to meet, or who works for your target company, ask her to sit with you!

Some organizations don't have a hospitality function. No problem....volunteer to start one. In essence, you are creating your own volunteer role. Do a web search to find out best practices for Hospitality Committee members. It will be easy to make an immediate difference in the organization, while you meet and make friends with everyone.

2. Membership Committee

The second opportunity is to volunteer for the Membership Committee. It's more work than Hospitality, but a secret source of opportunity for a job seeker. The Membership Committee is responsible for selling memberships to new members and making sure all current members renew. That gives you access to the entire database of your organization. You will know who everyone is, who they work for, their contact information, and so much more.

As a general rule, you're not allowed to use the database for personal gain or to try and sell products and services.

However, now you have an excuse to call up the president or the hiring manager of a company you want to work with and say, "Hello, Mr. Jones. I'm *calling from the AMA. Your membership is renewing in March. Could I come by your office for 15 minutes to update you on the benefits of membership and discuss upcoming programs?*" Perhaps you can ask him to become more active by attending the next meeting as your guest. Maybe he'd be open to speaking at an upcoming event, or hosting an industry social. In any case, use the opportunity to build a relationship while showcasing yourself as an active member of your professional community. There is practically no other way you can connect with leaders in your industry as comfortably and easily as this.

3. Public Relations Committee

The PR Committee is generally responsible for publishing press releases, news bulletins and calendar alerts about the organization and its events. You might also end up writing a newsletter or setting up media interviews. This will build your personal brand visibility, because your name will be on every press release you send, and they will then be picked up by Google search. It's also a very effective way to create or gain access to a database of journalists that you may end up contacting for a personal or business story. And it generally doesn't take too much of a time investment.

Actively Connect with Former Friends and Colleagues

Go through your phonebook, Rolodex (if you still have one), LinkedIn and email database and find former colleagues, and then reach out to them. Suggest coffee, lunch or a drink after work to catch up if they are local, or a call on their drive to or from work to chat when it is convenient for them. Find out what they are doing and update them on your recent accomplishments. Let them know that while you are fine with your current employer, you are seeking a new challenge that will excite and ignite you. Ask if they know anyone looking for a stellar candidate like you, or if they know about any openings in their company or elsewhere. Tell them you'd love to work with them if they ever have an opportunity where you can work as a team again.

By far, the top way people get hired is through a referral from someone who works for the hiring company. Ask your friend or colleague to forward your résumé to the person who would be your future boss, or the CEO, and to copy the VP of Human Resources.

Remember, people hire people they know, like and trust. Refresh them on your many skills and talents so you will be top of mind when a job opens up.

Network Through Your Alumni Association

One of the very best ways to network is through your college's alumni association. The Alumni Office can give you a list of all the alumni in your city or state, along with contact information. They may have an online database of alumni you can search by city, state, industry, employer, past employers, job title, and more.

Join the social media pages of your school and your school alumni association — focus on Facebook and Linked In. You can reach out through a post saying *"I'd like a referral to someone in XYZ Corporation. Can you help me reach someone in the XYZ department?"* You'll be amazed at the response.

Most alumni associations offer local events or socials; attend as many as possible. If there is no local alumni association where you live, start one. It's easy; just call the alumni office and tell them where you live and offer to start a local chapter. They will send you a whole packet of information, along with the database of all alumni in the region. Then email and call everyone on the list and ask to meet after work at 5:30 or 6:00 p.m. on a weekday at a bar or restaurant for a networking social or dinner. You will have an immediate bond with other alumni due to the power of affinity. You can set up your alumni contact database using MailChimp or Constant Contact to send out email invites and manage your invitations to attend and reservations on an Eventbrite page.

Network Through Churches, Temples, Religious, Family-oriented or Civic Organizations

All religious organizations are a great way to network. So are organizations that support your family members: PTA, band boosters, or athletic boosters for school organizations, Cub Scouts and Girl Scouts, and hundreds more.

Many civic or service organizations are dedicated to contributing to the community, and often their members and volunteers tend to be professionals with great contacts.

Rotary Clubs, Chambers of Commerce, Manufacturers' Associations and any other organization that represents your type of employer are great ways to network. Join them representing your current company, so you have an engagement platform. Your company may offer to pay for it, particularly if it is an organization that is relevant to your current position.

Conduct Interviews for a Book or Article or Paper You Are Writing

Everyone wants to feel special and have their opinions heard. An audacious technique is to contact the hiring manager or CEO or VP of Human Resources of a company you would like to work for and ask to interview them for a paper you are preparing. Make sure the request is legitimate. Plan to interview several different people and write a thoughtful article on LinkedIn, if you don't have another publishing platform like a blog or a legitimately forthcoming book. Come up with a theme that showcases your skills and expertise and ask their opinion about it.

In my case, as a career coach, it might be about their attitudes towards older workers, concern about turnover among millenials, their employee skills shortage, what internal training programs they offer, what benefits they offer. Perhaps ask about innovations they are using or evaluating in the recruiting function, their forecast for advanced technologies like IT, robotics, virtual reality, etc. that may change the nature of the workforce in the next five years, etc. You can easily come up with similar relevant concepts in your industry for the topic of your article.

Engage in an insightful conversation, subtly showcase your own knowledge and experience, and ask their opinions and respond and give appreciative feedback. Follow up with a thank you note. When you post the article on your blog or on LinkedIn, write an email with a link to the article to continue the conversation, and ask for their comment on LinkedIn. Then share the LinkedIn article on all your social media sites.

You will have established yourself as a thought leader, a bright and inquisitive professional who is on top of your game. That's the impression you want to create. You will have established a relationship that allows you to talk with an influential person in the company, and leverage that to enquire about how you can contribute to the success of the company in the future.

You're Not Unemployed, You're on a Sabbatical

The biggest challenge many unemployed professionals face is "What do you do for a living?" It makes many people so uncomfortable that they withdraw and don't network — which is a huge mistake. When you meet people casually or at a networking event, don't ever say you are unemployed. Either present the business card of your consulting credentials (we'll discuss that next), or say you are on a sabbatical from whatever your profession is.

A sabbatical is not a new concept; it appears in the Bible in several places. It derives from the Sabbath, the seventh day of the week, and generally is a period of rest and renovation every seven years. It means purposeful time spent to gain restoration. University professors traditionally received paid leave for one year every seven years for travel, research, or writing a thesis, paper or book.

In your case, you are on a sabbatical from a high-pressure job, deciding if you want to stay in the industry, or start a new career. Don't ever talk negatively about your former employer. But you can say, for example, "*I am evaluating my options as I am no longer challenged in my job*", "*I'm looking for a company with values more consistent with my own*", or "*I'm looking to work for an inspirational leader or management team that will allow me to better contribute my skills to a meaningful purpose.*"

On a job interview, you will of course discuss why you left your job, and you can talk about layoffs, RIFs, leadership changes, downsizing, etc. But you don't need to go into those details with casual acquaintances. Saying you are on a sabbatical implies that you are contemplative and reflective, rather than desperately looking for a job.

12

START YOUR OWN CONSULTING COMPANY

I believe that every mature professional should have your own consulting company, to serve as credentials when unemployed or looking or a job, and to be a Plan B in your career. It also covers employment gaps in your résumé. The earlier you start your company, the more credible it is. But it's never too late to start.

Legal Structure

You don't have to do anything other than print business cards and build a small four page website to set up a consulting company. In most states, you don't need to file for an LLC or incorporate if you use your own name and operate as a sole proprietorship. You may want to apply for a Fictitious Name Certificate for your business if you choose a name other than your own name. Check out the page on Corporations on your local state Secretary of State website for rules on sole proprietorships and taxation as these vary state-to-state.

If you decide to set up a corporation or LLC and opt to go through a lawyer, expect to pay between $1,000 and $2,000. You can generally file your organization documents yourself for just the filing fees, but it varies by state.

Another great option is to use a service like Legal Zoom (*LegalZoom.com*) that will file all the organization documents for you for a couple of hundred dollars. I am not a financial or legal advisor, so you should seek professional help in this area.

The Benefits of Your Own Company

The key benefit of setting up your own consulting company is that you can interface with potential employers as a professional peer rather than as a job applicant. As a consultant, you are able to reach out to the hiring manager or

CEO, while as a job seeker, the organization tries to limit contact through the HR department.

In the great majority of cases, you won't ever generate any revenue through your company, and probably won't need a sale tax certificate, occupancy permit or FEIN, as you will file taxes under your own Social Security number as a Sole Proprietor.

There are great tax benefits for working out of a home office. If you work out of a bona fide home office, and do not have another office location provided by an employer, you can deduct a substantial amount of home office expenses to reduce your taxable income, which will save you thousands in taxes.

You can deduct a pro-rata portion of rent, insurance, utilities, maintenance, repairs and other operating expense based on the size of your home office or exclusive workspace, compared to the square footage of the rest of your house. So if you live in a 1,500 square foot rental home, and have an office that is 10' x 15', that is 150 square feet, so you can deduct 10% of your annual housing expenses. If you look at monthly housing expenses of $2,500 per month, that comes out to $3,000 per year.

On top of that, you can fully deduct unreimbursed business expenses, such as your mobile phone, home fax or phone, equipment such as computers and printers (you may have to depreciate larger capital expenses), broadband internet, computer software, services, and repairs, office supplies, and any other unreimbursed expenses.

Home office deductions are trickier if you own your home, and you may face tax complications if you deduct home office mortgage and property taxes and then sell your home. The IRS is very strict about home office deductions, so check with your tax accountant. Recent tax law changes may affect this also. You may only be able to deduct home office expenses if your business makes a profit, so many self-employed professionals arrange to have deductible expenses slightly less than their gross revenues, so they can make a tiny but important profit after home office deductions. The 2017 tax law made changes in home office deductions for employees, and some of those changes may affect you also. Check with your accountant or CPA about this tricky topic.

Working For a Start Up

With time to spare and while looking for a new job, you may be approached by young start-up companies seeking your help to get them to the next stage.

They never have money and will ask you to work for no pay. It's a better use of your time than watching TV all day. But realize that less than 10% of start-ups make it, so your efforts may be in vain. On the other hand, you can add the company to your client list, and you will have something interesting and forward-looking to talk about with other professionals or on a job interview.

Negotiate your consulting rate at the beginning, along with the number of hours you can dedicate to the project. You can say something like, "*My consulting rate is $100 per hour, and I can dedicate 10 hours a week for the next 5 months to help you get up and going. That's 200 hours, or the equivalent of $20,000. I know you can't pay that, but let's make an agreement that if the company is successful, or gains equity investment or other financing, my consulting fees will be converted to equity at the same rate as the new investors, and in the equity amount of $20,000. If the company doesn't make it for any reason, then you owe me nothing.*" In this way you have a piece of the pie if the company is successful. Make sure you write this agreement up in a simple contract, and add that any continued involvement in the company will extend the agreement on a pro-rata basis at the monthly rate of $4,000 per month or something like that. You may end up working more than 10 hours per week, as start-ups can be all-consuming, but at least you will have established your value and you have an agreed-up equity role. Don't invest your time without the agreement, or you will probably end up regretting it.

Buy Your Domain Name

Now is the time to register your own professional name as a domain name before anyone else does. I bought *www.DianeHuth.com* more than a decade ago. I don't do anything with it, but have it directed to my bio page on my business website. You may not be able to get your name for your website without modifying it to add a middle name, middle initial, or descriptor, which may also serve as the name of your consulting business. Make sure you secure the domain name with a .com extension (not .biz or .us) for your business before finalizing the name. Your company could then be named John Doe Consulting Engineers, for example, and your domain name could be *www.JohnDoe.com*, *www.JohnXDoe.com*, *www.JohnDoeEngineers.com* or *www.JohnDoeEng.com*. You want your own name to be prominent and a description of what you do, but not so long that it won't fit on your business card.

I strongly recommend you use GoDaddy for all your domain and web services. I have had nothing but the most outstanding customer service from them 24/7 by knowledgeable techs who live in the United States. They are the only web domain and web service company you ever will need.

It'll cost you less than $20 a year to own your domain name. They often offer discounts for services — right now they are offering a promotion for $1.00 for a new annual domain registration, and $1.00 per month for your GoCentral website building platform, which includes several professional email addresses.

Get Your Personalized Company Email

You will want to have your email with your name at your company email address, such as *John@JohnDoe.com* or *John@JohnDoeEngineering.com*. Whenever you spell out a multi-word domain name, I suggest you use a capital first letter for each word to make it easy to read. Computers don't care if a website in spelled in caps or low case and it makes it so much easier for everyone else to understand.

Create A Simple Website

I suggest you build a small three or four page professional website to serve as a digital résumé and portfolio. Your Home page should talk about what you can do for your client. Showcase your skills, your business philosophy, and your brand promise — how you can benefit the visitor, who may be your potential client. The second page should be a Bio or About page which tells your story and highlights your skills, achievements, education and capabilities. Have a great studio photo of yourself on this page.

A third page is your Credentials or Services page, which will talk about the services you offer, and will show client logos, and examples of work that you have done throughout your career. It will become your online professional portfolio. You will want to list all your former employers and any customers you served in prior jobs. You can also perform volunteer or pro bono work through your company, and list them as clients.

The last page will be your Contact Us page. Make sure you have a form for easy communication, and all your contact information. Avoid listing your home address as you don't want job seekers or potential customers or vendors showing up unannounced at your front door. You may work from your home office, or list your address at a tech incubator, which may rent seats for $50 a month. Alternatively, rent a post office box from a local UPS Store and use their address.

The GoDaddy Go Central website builder is very easy and intuitive to use, and you can build a professional and attractive website in just a few hours. Then it just takes minutes to update it at no additional cost. For step-by-step instructions and desktop capture images of the process, check out *BRAND YOU To Master Your Social Media*, Chapter 20. If you need help building your site, contact me at *Diane@BrandYouGuide.com* or find a freelancer to build your website on *Upwork.com, Fiverr.com*, or other source. It should cost around $500 for a freelancer to write your copy, create your branding, and build a simple website. Save time and money by laying out the website you envision using PowerPoint and writing draft copy and providing the logos and photos and other content you will need.

Create Your Company Branding

You will need to select a branding look and feel, which you can establish based on the website template you select. You may also want to hire a graphic designer to create your branding, which will include a logo, color scheme, fonts, design elements, look and feel. Your branding will be used in your website, business card, letterhead, LinkedIn page and anything else you can create to showcase you and your skills. I have had great luck with *99Designs.com*, and also with *Upwork.com*, where I hire a lot of freelance services.

Create a Photo Business Card

The final thing you need to set up your consulting company or start to look for a job is an attractive, impactful and memorable business card that will help interviewers remember you after a long job fair or a day of multiple interviews. You will use your professional business card even after you get a job and have a business card from an employer.

Vistaprint is Your One-Stop Shop

You don't need to hire a graphic designer to create a fabulous business card, just go to Vistaprint for a one-stop design and print solution. Click on Business Cards to see more than 4,000 different design options.

At the bottom of the left-hand Menu box, select "Use your photos & logos" to find hundreds of great designs that will showcase your photo. You should expect to pay around $25 for 500 full color business cards.

There are many other places you can design and print business cards, including UPS stores and office supply stores. Most offer comparable pricing to Vistaprint.

Follow These Tips to Create Your Own Card:

+ Prominently feature your company name, logo and your photo.
+ Use your professional email.
+ For Title, use Principal, General Manager, CEO or Founder.
+ Select a rich, colorful or dark-colored design which integrates with your overall branding, rather than a more common mainly-white card — it will be more memorable.
+ Print a full color back for your card.
+ Select extra thick paper, or another heavy weight or distinctive paper stock, such as metallic, textured, pearlized, to stand out from other cards.
+ Consider upscale printing techniques, like embossing, gold foil stamping, or 3D varnish to be distinctive.
+ Select one or two professional fonts that you want to use consistently

on your professional branding materials; a bold headline font and a body copy font. Use these on your cards, on your résumé, website, and more. Your website template may have the fonts you want to use in all your branding.

- Consider rounded corners as an option to stand out.

Print 250 or 500 cards — they should cost around $25 for full color on standard stock, up to $75 or $100 with lots of fancy options. It's an important investment in your professional image, so create your cards now and always carry them with you everywhere.

Create a Memorable Image That Links to Your Name

Remember you are a brand and like a brand, your name and image should be as memorable as possible. If your name is a color, use that color as a color signature…. Mr. Brown, White, Gray, Silver, Green, etc. I met a woman who was running for an elected office, and her last name was Rojo…..that's "Red" in Spanish. She wore only red, nothing else. She was distinctive and memorable and reinforced her personal branding. I worked with Mr. Green, and he always wore green and used only green pens for writing, reinforcing his name branding. A friend whose last name is Diamond has a tasteful image of a diamond on his card; a family member whose last name is Keyes uses the image of a golden key on his card. Look for distinctive features of your name, first or last, to exploit in your self-branding.

Branding Consistency is Key

As a brand, you need to create a consistently positive image. Make sure you're consistent in how you present yourself, using your photo, email signature, name, fonts and color scheme. Your résumé and online image today will be available to employers during online searches for the next ten years or more, so create a strong and memorable brand presence starting with your business card and website.

MASTER YOUR SOCIAL MEDIA PRESENCE

I've written a whole book on this subject — *BRAND YOU! Master Your Social Media* — so I can only summarize some of the key points that are the most relevant to the mature professional.

I believe there are six key social media sites that you should use to brand yourself professionally. While you may think of sites like Facebook, Twitter and Pinterest as fun social engagement tools to stay in touch with family and friends, they can become powerful assets in your career development and job search. Likewise, if used incorrectly, they can torpedo your career and prevent you from landing your dream job.

Key social media site
You can post content, ask questions, follow, comment, connect for research, search employees for jobs

Highlight your actions
Show photos of appropriate personal events, school or professional activities, follow and LIKE people and firms of interest , share professional content, quotes, images

Marketing & PR
Journalists and bloggers post all their content on Twitter, important in the marketing community, follow and like key content providers

Key social media site
Growing in popularity, often used for corporate content

Great source of images
And visual posts. Follow key industry trends and post insightful content on other sites, brand contests

Marketing & PR
Subscribe to channels of market leaders, potential employers, industry associations to get notices of new content, great for discussion during interviews

© 2016 Superhero Branding and Marketing, Inc

We'll review the first three only — due to available space.

LinkedIn — Your Number One Job Hunting Resource

One of the first things your prospective employers will do is to look at your LinkedIn page — and see what it says about you professionally. According to one study, 94% of recruiters and human resource (HR) professionals name LinkedIn as the essential source for recruiting. LinkedIn is where you'll build and promote your professional profile, job history, education, affiliations, and so much more. If you don't have a LinkedIn page yet, sign up today. If you have a page already, update it with current information — it will walk you step-by-step through many of the options available. And of course list your contact information, including email and phone number.

Why LinkedIn?

Basic LinkedIn services are free, and a basic free account generally is adequate if you are employed. But if you are actively seeking a new job, you might consider upgrading to a Premium account which gives you access to hidden profiles and the ability to send InMail directly to any LinkedIn member even if you are not currently connected to them. LinkedIn has recently introduced the Career Plan, tailored for job seekers, at $30 per month. It may well be worth the investment if it helps you land your next job. LinkedIn is a powerful tool to network and reach out to potential employers or business colleagues you wouldn't be able to reach otherwise.

LinkedIn is a great networking and self-promotion tool, where colleagues can endorse you for specific skills, and you can show how savvy you are through the number of connections you have. But it can be much more than that. Today you can also post photos, comments, questions, blog posts, skills, presentations, white papers, and more. You can create an online portfolio on LinkedIn instantly viewable by everyone — for no charge. You can engage with other professionals by answering their questions or responding to and commenting on their posts and articles. This will make you stand out from other job candidates. LinkedIn should be your number one priority in your job search.

LinkedIn has perfected their site to the point where I suggest you build your LinkedIn profile *before* you create your résumé. LinkedIn will walk you step-by-step through every aspect of your career credentials, and prompt you if you are missing anything, such as employment dates or titles. If you complete your LinkedIn profile first, you have a great start on creating your powerful résumé later on.

Partial Listing of Features or Products To Make Your Personal Brand Shine:

+ **Create Your Profile** — Your first step is to create a free account and build out your basic profile. Use your professional photo that you use on all your job search materials. A great photo is key, as recruiters actively view your photos for insights into your employability. You can add a background image if desired, as long as it doesn't detract from your profile photo.

+ **Headline** — Choose a headline that clearly states who you are and what you do, and what you can do for an employer. This is a key search tool for recruiters looking for qualified job candidates, so make sure your headline and description are filled with searchable keywords and phrases.

+ **Contact and Personal Information** — Ensure that a recruiter or hiring manager can find you and contact you quickly and effortlessly. Fill this section out completely. I suggest you use your permanent professional email address and not a school or business address. You can link social media pages here, and much more.

+ **Education** — You will be prompted to enter details of your education, step-by-step, and they will be arranged in the appropriate reverse chronological order — most recent fist, older information on the bottom. Easy as pie. Your alumni network is one of your key assets, and a great way to connect instantly with many other mature professionals in leadership positions. Make sure you take advantage of your alumni network on LinkedIn.

+ **Employment** — Again you will be prompted to fill in details of employment, which will be arranged in reverse chronological order. Use keywords and focus on accomplishments rather than just a job description. A word about your LinkedIn employment profile and résumé: You must be rigorously honest and consistent; no cheating and no exaggeration. Make sure your LinkedIn profile mirrors your résumé. All this information is archived online for anyone to see, and any inconsistencies will pop up instantly. Your online résumé will become a public document that is cached online, so you must be totally honest and upfront about your information.

• **Invite People to Connect** — LinkedIn is a great way to connect with former colleagues at companies you worked for in the past, and they can be a valuable source of job leads. Connect to everyone you know still working in your former companies and also all your former colleagues. With the decades of work experience we bring to the table, this can be a substantial network to tap into.

• **Build Your Connections** — LinkedIn will ask you for access to all your email accounts, matching your contacts to other LinkedIn members, and suggest that you connect via an invitation they will send on your behalf. Just click the invite, and you will start gaining connections quickly and easily. As a mature professional, this is your competitive advantage! You have decades of experience and thousands of professional contacts to build out your contact listing in no time at all.

• **Gaining Endorsements and Recommendations** You want people to endorse you for your skills. Your extensive universe of professional connections makes it so easy to gain endorsements. LinkedIn will search out key words in your profile and suggest endorsement topics spontaneously to your connections. They also make it easy to get recommendations. There is actually a place to request such recommendations on your LinkedIn page. Click and request your recommendation. A simple strategy is to recommend them first! Just review all your contacts and write a short but glowing recommendation or endorsement about those who know the quality of your work — a couple of sentences is enough — and submit in online. In return, the majority will give *you* a recommendation without asking.

• **Create Posts** — These are quick messages of a timely nature, often with a call to action — notices about upcoming events or requests for information, invitations to apply for a job, etc. They can include images with insightful headlines, memes, quotes, etc. You can share posts from others that are relevant to your professional life. Here is where you can ask the LinkedIn community for introductions to key contacts at your desired company or ask for information about a target employer or industry.

+ **Post Articles** — You can post longer thoughtful articles of professional interest, often several pages long, accompanied by an image. You can include links to photos or videos or additional information. These are evergreen posts, meaning they will be viewed for a long period of time. I have articles and posts from years ago that are still being seen and liked. Re-purpose reports you have written in the past to create insightful content or create a new post with topical content. Your years of experience and your unique insights should make this an easy way to showcase your expertise and extensive credentials. Write as though it is a free instant blog.

+ **Jobs** — The Jobs icon on the menu bar allows you to search companies and individuals anywhere. You can select a range of search criteria, including individual name, company name, industry, current employees, former employees, market or geography, job titles, education, experience level and much more. This is why you need a great headline loaded with keywords. Recruiters will search for keywords and may find *you* more easily with a well-written LinkedIn profile.

+ **Messaging** — You can send instant messages to anyone in your community quickly with a single click, and likewise receive messages from anyone in your network. You will also automatically receive alerts about events — birthdays, job changes, work anniversaries, posts made, etc.

+ **InMail** — This is a premium service that requires a paid plan to allow you to message people outside your own network — such as potential employers and many CEOs. It also unmasks some senior executives whose contact is hidden on the regular platform. This can be a key reason to subscribe to a paid premium plan.

+ **Groups** — You can join and follow many different LinkedIn groups, which are important to expand your network and optimize your job search. Join your alumni groups, professional trade association groups, or groups that reflect a professional interest. You can use this platform to message members to help gain contacts or insights for your job search. Recruiters often check the groups that you may be following.

+ **Videos** — LinkedIn has hundreds of informational videos, many created by members, that can provide a wealth of information. They are free. Check them out.

- **SlideShare** — This is a forum which allows you to post PowerPoint presentations, infographics, white papers or other documents of useful professional information which you are willing to share freely with the online community. These presentations are evergreen, meaning they will be relevant forever or for a long time. Do you have a presentation you have prepared for a conference, training program, or industry overview that you can repurpose? A good SlideShare presentation may garner thousands of views over time and can establish you as an expert.

- **Salaries** — LinkedIn is a great source of information about salaries to help in your job search. It can provide a general range of salaries based on your desired job title. If you provide them with your current salary and company, LinkedIn will tailor a market analysis which will be much more specific.

- **So Much More** — There are many more tools available on LinkedIn, with new ones added every day. Go step-by-step to build your expanded profile using this list. You will soon have a powerful LinkedIn profile that will set you up for job search success. Click on the Career Interests button to indicate to recruiters that you are interested in job opportunities and see who reaches out to you. You can also search and connect with the companies you want to work for and contact the hiring manager via LinkedIn.

Facebook – Show How You Invest Your Time and Energy

 Half of all potential employers will look at your Facebook page as part of the screening process, according to *CareerBuilder*. It will tell them who you are as a person — what your interests are, how you spend your time, who you associate with, how you express yourself in writing, your political affiliation, whether or not you are married, or if you are a partier, a jock or a couch potato.

If you don't have a Facebook account yet, get one. If you don't exhibit basic social media skills, a potential employer will assume you don't master even basic technology, and it may prevent you from being considered for a job.

So what are they going to find on YOUR Facebook page today?

Search through the last three months of your Facebook posts and evaluate yourself as an employer will. Are you family-oriented, or do you hang out with friends? Do you drink and go to nightclubs and party hard every weekend? What values do you express in your posts? Are many of your posts political diatribes — for either party? Or do you engage in positive or altruistic activities such as volunteer work or church activities? Do you walk in charity events, belong to the Y, or participate in community or volunteer activities? Do you care for and spend time with parents, family members, your spouse or children? Potential employers will look at your posts with these questions in mind to understand you as a person.

You should also stay clear of political posts and comments on your Facebook page. Half of all Americans belong to the other party, so you can't afford to offend them!

Employers are generally looking for a stable mature adult with some family responsibilities so they know you will take the job seriously and won't quit on a whim. A potential employer may invest tens of thousands of dollars in training you for the job, and they want to feel comfortable that you are a reliable, serious employee who will fit into the company culture.

3 Steps to Manage Your Facebook Postings

1. Go through your own Facebook timeline and delete any photos or posts that will not look good to a potential employer. To remove objectionable posts, highlight the little down arrow on the top right corner of the post, and click "delete" or "hide from timeline."
2. If you are tagged in someone else's unflattering post, ask them to hide or delete the post in which you are tagged.
3. Actively start posting positive messages and images that a potential employer will appreciate. Post inspirational messages. Talk about positive things you are doing. Post about successes at work, in your professional associations, or charity events you are involved in. Make posts that show your value system. Post about family members and business or community leaders you admire. Share positive stats, information, or images relating to your profession. But be authentic. Let your Facebook page sing your praises to a potential employer.

Twitter — Follow Thought Leaders to Become One

Do you Tweet? If you don't, it may not be too late to start — or to at least follow other people on Twitter.

Prospective employers may look at your Twitter feed and see what you're talking about. They're going to see if your posts are insightful or silly, if you follow thoughtful leaders and journalists or shallow Hollywood celebrities. Use Twitter to showcase your skills and strengths, not to show weaknesses. It is also important to discretely indicate that you are tech savvy — a key trait you want to communicate to a future employer.

Most people think of using Twitter for fun, but it can play a very important role in your career. Most journalists use Twitter to post their stories and interact with followers. Follow a dozen or so important thought leaders in your desired industry, commenting insightfully every time they post a new story. You will go far in your own professional networking, and you will impress potential employers with your commitment to and knowledge of your field.

You will need to have a Twitter account if you work in marketing, journalism, public relations, and many other fields. If you want to get a story published, you need to follow the key writers you wish to engage with through their Twitter feeds. For example, if you want to place a story in *Forbes*, follow the writers and editors who cover your industry or topics in that publication. Start following them on Twitter, LIKE and SHARE their stories, and post insightful and favorable comments on every story. Soon you will be chatting with key writers like old friends, so when you want to place that story in *Forbes*, you have a colleague that you can easily contact.

Register These Additional Social Media Pages

While LinkedIn, Facebook, and Twitter are the top social media sites you will need for your job search, you can use several other social media and digital tools for promoting your professional life. Take a few moments now to register these accounts in your same professional name so you have a consistent social media presence.

Pinterest

You may want to have a professional Pinterest page. It's not just for women and personal fun anymore. Create a professional account with boards that profile your professional heroes, give motivational quotes, state key insights about your profession, etc. LIKE each pin you post, then follow everyone whose pin you post, and they will probably follow you — which allows you to build your social media following. You can even link your Pinterest page directly to your Facebook page or Twitter account and share pins directly to those social media sites. Already use Pinterest and don't want a second account? Create a board just for professional or job-related content, and link that specific board to your professional Facebook page.

YouTube

Communication today is shifting to video, so take the time now to register your own professional YouTube channel. You don't even need to post anything on your own channel today to benefit your job search. Simply subscribe to the channel of every company or brand you want to work for as well as their competitors. For example, if you want to work for Procter and Gamble (P&G) on Pampers, subscribe to Pampers' YouTube Channel, and also to Huggies' and LUV's channels. Every time one of them posts a new video, you'll get an email alert so you can immediately watch the video. You can LIKE it, SHARE it, and post comments on the page that will be seen by Pampers' marketing team. You can send an email commenting on the new video to the recruiter or hiring manager at P&G that you want to connect with. At your upcoming job interview, you can say "I found your new Olympics video campaign was very motivational and right on target," or make an insightful comment about a competitor's campaign. This shows them that you are paying attention and have done your research well.

Google+

I personally don't use Google+ much, but many business professionals and companies do. The key benefits include immediate listing of your content on Google, and a higher

Google ranking for your page and content than through organic search. If you register a YouTube page, you will automatically be assigned a Google+ page. To put it in perspective, there are more active Google+ accounts than Twitter accounts, so you understand the scale it offers. Just duplicate your Facebook or LinkedIn posts on G+ using a free platform like HootSuite.

14

BUILD A POWERFUL RÉSUMÉ

One of the most powerful tools in your job-hunting toolbox is a strong and effective résumé. It will make or break your job search, so you must craft a strong, persuasive and enticing one. You want a résumé that HR will like, your future boss will be intrigued with, and the search engines and web crawlers will find and showcase.

If you're an active professional and have changed jobs fairly frequently, you probably know the key points of crafting a persuasive résumé. If you haven't changed jobs in years, you may want to update your skills. If you're starting your career now, read with care to get up to date fast.

According to *BeHiring.com*, the average recruiter conducting a preliminary screening will spend just six to seven seconds reviewing your résumé, so it's important that the four key items he is looking for jump out immediately:

+ Job titles
+ Name of employers
+ Start and end dates of employment or years of work
+ Education

I wrote a whole book about how to prepare your résumé — *BRAND YOU! Create Your Powerful Résumé* — available on Amazon in e-book format. It's also extensively covered in my first book *BRAND YOU! To Land Your Dream Job*, available in both paperback and e-book formats. So here are just the highlights, as there's just not enough room to cover this topic in full detail.

Let's start with the hard copy résumé first. This is the résumé you will present to a potential employer at a face-to-face meeting.

Six Sections to a Great Résumé

A great résumé has six key sections, presented in a specific order. Make sure you understand the purpose and formatting for each one. Here is how these should be organized from top to bottom.

1. Name and Contact Information

Use your professional name at the top of the résumé, in bold caps or otherwise highlighted so it jumps off the page and is easy to see. Underneath that, list your contact information — your professional email address, your phone number formatted 123-456-7890, rather than the customary (123) 456-7890, to appear more contemporary. You can add a LinkedIn address, or the address of your online portfolio. Embed the link in your document if you will distribute it online or submit it to an online site. Add a 1-line footer for all pages, with your name, email, phone, and page number.

Have two versions of your résumé, one listing the city where you live, and one without. No one is going to mail you a letter when they can send an email instead, so leave off the street address and just list the city and state. An out-of-town address may cause a potential employer to discard your résumé to avoid relocation expense. If you are applying for an out-of-town position, use the résumé without the city listed. For an in-town job, use the résumé listing the city so the recruiter knows that relocation won't be an issue.

Make sure you have a modern email address, and that means Gmail or an email from your own website. Old email addresses signal your age and lack of technical ability and peg you as old or old fashioned and not with it technologically. So you can keep your legacy AOL, Yahoo, People PC or cable company email addresses for your personal communication, but get a free Gmail address to prevent subtle age discrimination. The Gmail address should be your professional name, with initials, middle name, dots, etc. to create a Gmail address that is easy to find by a recruiter searching for your name in his database. Alternatively, you could have your email from your consulting company or your own domain name — *John@ JohnSmithRealtor.com.*

2. Career Objective

You need to tell a prospective employer exactly what kind of a job you are looking for and in what field. If you don't have a stated objective, the employer may not know what you want to do and will go on to the next résumé.

I had a great client with a lot of unrelated work experience, and her résumé didn't have a job objective. She had worked as a nanny for five years, while putting herself through college to earn a business degree in marketing. So the logical question was "*Are you applying for a job as a nanny?*" Of course not, she wanted a job in marketing. Without clearly stating that goal, a prospective employer would not make sense of her résumé.

I likewise coached an experienced IT professional with vast experience in many different technical fields, currently employed as an IT Director by a $4 Billion retailer with hundreds of stores. In discussing his career goal, I pushed him to clarify his objectives, which he had never put in words before. The right job for him was to become CTO or CIO for a small or mid-size company. It added great clarity and confidence when he "claimed" that role and listed it clearly in the Objective section of his résumé.

So write a very specific job objective, such as:

- Senior-level position in brand management for a leading CPG company
- Staff Accountant, with focus on accounts receivable and collections
- Senior Account Executive position in a B2C digital marketing agency
- Executive Director for a non-profit health organization serving the local community
- Production Supervisor for a thermoform plastics manufacturer

Then you will enhance that objective by stating some of your relevant skills that make you a perfect match for the job, so the recruiter can visualize what you can do for the company. This is where all those years of experience pay off in spades!

But that's not all. You need to express your career objective while showcasing your skills and experience and then help the recruiter visualize what you will do for the company. To do that, you restate or synthesize the job description using the same keywords so your résumé will be matched in the online ATS system.

Therefore, the full job description might read:

> Senior-level position in brand management for a leading CPG company, utilizing my 20+ years of experience in all aspects of consumer-focused marketing and product management for leading Fortune 100 companies, to spearhead the development of new product introductions and ramp up consumer engagement programs.

Here is an example from a former CEO with 40 years of experience:

> Senior subsea engineering, manufacturing and equipment industry leader and innovator, seeking affiliation with a firm where I can provide organizational and technological leadership, growing and mentoring a strong team based on extensive experience in all aspects of offshore and subsea technology, strong industry relationships, and recognized industry expertise as evidenced by 11 patents and extensive publications.

Focus on what you can do for the company in a forward-looking manner. Don't lean on just your decades of experience; instead, discuss what that experience brings to your future employer so they can envision you in the job and how you will contribute to meeting the company's goals. And don't say "*40 years of experience*"; you will automatically be considered too old. Refer to characteristic like "executive level," "senior level", "C-suite", etc.

This section should clearly state how your credentials exactly match the job description by mirroring the wording of the job posting. That's right, I said "mirror." By this I mean use the exact same words and phrases as in the job posting. This is important because many of the jobs you will be applying for are listed online, and recruiters and headhunters use key word searches to find and vet prospective candidates. By mirroring the wording of the job posting and requirements, your résumé will match the keywords in the search criteria, and the computer should flag your résumé as a good match.

You should have one basic résumé with your most desired career objective which you will place on LinkedIn. But you will need to customize the objective section of *each* résumé you send out to the posted job and company.

3. Summary of Skills or Overview

This is a brief summary of relevant skills you offer and clarifies why the company should hire you. Often, employers won't read past this section, so you need to give them compelling reasons why you are the right candidate for the job.

Create a brief summary of skills and qualifications in a 2- or 3-column bulleted format. Avoid the fluff. *"Good team player"* and *"hardworking and motivated"* are throwaway words in this section. Use words that clearly communicate a tangible or unique skill, talent, capability or credential.

SIGNATURE STRENGTHS		
HR Development & Infrastructure Benefit Analysis & Administration Strategic Planning & Project Management Contracts Administration & Negotiations Recruitment & Talent Acquisition	Health & Welfare Vendor Selection 401k Plans Audit & Non-Discrimination Open Enrollment Workforce Analysis & Planning Onboarding Process	**Industry Experience:** Construction & Drilling Energy Manufacturing Oil & Gas

Here's another example:

PROFESSIONAL SUMMARY

- Bachelor's degree in criminal justice
- Career coach and employment advisor
- Extensive non-profit and entrepreneurial experience
- Supervisor of homeless center for at-risk individuals
- Recruitment and supervision of mental health professionals
- Excellent track record of recruiting passionate volunteers
- Agent and manger to athletes, entertainers and artists
- Developed innovative alternative educational programs
- Management experience of more than $8 million of assets
- Extensive training and mentoring background
- Program conception, design, start-up and management
- Team builder, collaborator, stakeholder coordination
- Strong background working with diverse populations
- Outstanding interpersonal and communication abilities
- Ability to simultaneously coordinate multiple projects
- U.S. Army veteran

If you are personalizing the résumé to a specific job description, you may want to include a comparison between the job requirements on the posting and show how you meet or exceed them. Use the exact language of the job posting to highlight your relevant qualifications.

Personalize this list for each job you apply for to ensure the skills match the list of job requirements. Be concise and consider arranging the list in columns like this example to save space.

Sometime people put this section at the end of their résumé, also in columns or in a grid. Either way works, as long as it is short, clear and contains just key phrases and not a lot of editorial fluff.

Desired Credentials for CMO Position		
Category	Requirement	My Credentials
Education	Min BA, MBA preferred	BA Business Administration, MBA concentration in Entrepreneurship
Professional Experience	Min 10 years experience	18 years progressive experience in marketing, sales and product development
Functional Experience	Marketing, Sales, General Management	6 years Brand Marketing, 3 years B2B Sales, 5 years B2C Sales, 4 years Product Development,
Management Experience	Director or VP Experience	CMO 6 years, Internal Management Committee Member, currently supervise team of 47
Certifications	PMP	PMP Certification 2014
Language Skills	Fluent English, Bilingual desired	Native English speaker, fluent in Spanish, beginning Chinese

4. Education

Depending upon the amount of your professional experience, the 4th section of your résumé will probably be Experience. However, if you received an advanced degree or graduated from a very prestigious university, you might want to start with Education in a very concise section consisting of just a few lines.

This list of professional education should be in reverse chronological order, with most recent education first, and oldest education last. At this point in your career, you want to highlight just the key data:

+ The degree, major and minor — for example *B.A. in Business Administration, Major in Marketing, Minor in French.* Leave off the year if you graduated more than 20 years ago.
+ The name of the university, city and state — *Middlebury College, Middlebury VT*
+ Special awards and recognition — *Cum Laude, class valedictorian, Dean's List 6 semesters, member of Phi Beta Kappa Honor Society,* etc. Keep it short to only the most important information.

Keep it tight and concise. If you can get it down to just a half-dozen lines, you can put it above the Experience section to check off that box. If you didn't graduate from college, put Education below the Experience section, and list school name, city, state and area of study, but don't mention degree. You could mention the number of credit hours earned to save an uncomfortable question about whether or not you graduated. Eliminate the years you attended or graduated to discourage age bias.

5. Professional Experience

Your Professional Experience also should be listed in reverse chronological order, oldest at the bottom, most recent at the top. Focus on the most recent 10–15 years.

Organize your listing either by company name first, or by title, depending upon which is more impressive. If you worked for a prestigious company like IBM or Coca-Cola, list the company first. If you worked for an unknown company, you may want to list your title first, then the company name, and a one or two-word description so the recruiter knows it was a CPA firm, law office, construction company, IT service company, etc.

Whichever format you choose, be consistent throughout the résumé. Add the city and state (use the 2-letter state abbreviation), and the years of employment on the first line if possible. Don't add the months of employment — it's just too much information and adds unnecessary clutter. Alternatively, don't list dates at all; list the number of years, or number of years and months you worked each job. Format the document so the years end up flush right, easy to see during a quick scan of the résumé. This line of the résumé should probably be bold or underlined or both to easily stand out.

On the next line, add a brief one-sentence description of key job responsibilities or functions, and brief information about the company or division if needed for clarity. You may want to clarify your department or division, number of direct and indirect reports, budgets managed, or revenue of company or of your position. Avoid company jargon or company-specific terms. Examples might include:

- Leading digital marketing agency serving 50+ B2B and B2C small and medium sized companies, with revenue of $22 million, staff of 44, with 7 direct reports.
- Thermoformed plastics manufacturer serving wide range of clients in the Midwest, sales of $44 million, operating 4 facilities in 3 states.
- Leading credit union serving the petroleum refining industry, with 52 branches in 4 Gulf States serving 32,000 consumers and small businesses, offering a full portfolio of financial services.

Then list in bullet form your three to five key quantifiable accomplishments — not activities or responsibilities — starting with action verbs in the past tense for prior jobs, and in present tense for your current job. If possible, add a time frame or period. Check out these examples:

- Spearheaded 12% revenue growth through new CRM system in FY 2014
- Increased customer count by 500 new members (+8%) in a 4-month period
- Reduced quality control rejects by 17% through implementation of a vendor pre-certification program over 2 years
- Generated $500,000 of direct sales of computer peripherals in first year
- Exceeded sales quota by 37% in 2016
- Received President's Award as top 5% of national sales force in 2012
- Created and posted 87 new social media and blog posts to support line expansion

Present information in this section consistently and attractively, with the job title, employers' names, and years or length of employment easy to find in a quick scan. These are the three employment items any recruiter will look for first, so they need to pop out quickly during an initial seven-second scan.

At this point of your career, you may want to keep these job listings very brief, with the most current or relevant positions in more detail showcasing quantifiable accomplishments, with the listings becoming progressively briefer the older they are. But keep them brief; better three impactful accomplishments than a laundry list of 10 items for each employer.

You may want to summarize all relevant experience that is more than 10 or 15 years old, unless it is directly related to the skills needed for the job you are applying for. This section could read: *Prior Professional Experience — progressively increasing responsibility starting as Management Trainee with steady promotions to Factory Manager. Industry experience includes petrochemicals, injection molding, glass manufacturing, and tire manufacturing, for leading employers including Firestone, Owens Corning, and 3M.* Keep it short and sweet, and don't mention dates.

Avoid part-time or in-between jobs, or positions that don't add stature to your credentials. You want to focus on recent or current relevant work experience.

Having your own consulting company as a concurrent employer may help to mask employment voids so your résumé can focus on walking the recruiter through your story to show how your background and experience has prepared you to solve their problems today.

6. Skills and Expertise — Optional as Appropriate

◆ **Computer Skills** List your computer skills here — these are critical in today's market. Basic knowledge of the Microsoft Office suite is essential, but not everyone is skilled at Publisher or Access, so highlight these if you know them. Mastery of the Adobe Creative Suite is very impressive — Photoshop, Illustrator, InDesign are important, as well as any video editing and web development software including WordPress if you want to work in business, marketing or creative fields. Also list any specialty software expertise you have, CAD/CAM, GIS, banking/finance software, QuickBooks, PMP or Project Management software, etc. If working in IT, include a grid with the various programs and languages you excel in. Don't mention overly basic programs or applications like Google, Facebook, LinkedIn, or social media sites, unless you are a certified expert in them. This Computer Skills section is critical to help you overcome concerns about whether you have the tech skills needed in today's workplace.

◆ **Foreign Languages** List languages other than English, and indicate your mastery level, whether you are fluent, intermediate, or would be considered a beginner.

◆ **Certifications and Licenses** List any certifications that are relevant to your business, such as PMP (Project Management), CPA, Insurance and Financial Services certifications (Series 6 license or mortgage broker license), Cordon Bleu, etc. You may want to add these to your Education section instead if they are impressive or essential to your career.

◆ **Awards** If you have relevant and impressive awards or prizes other than those listed under Education, list these here.

◆ **Professional Associations** List memberships in your professional associations, focusing on Board positions or volunteer roles. Virtually every industry has one or more professional or trade associations, and you should join, participate and volunteer.

+ **Military Service** Provide branch, rank, job assignment, specialized training, key assignments, awards and recognition, etc. Explain current status — *"Retired as Captain June 2018, honorable discharge March 2015, currently in Arizona National Guard,"* etc.

+ **Non-Job-Related Activities** List only key volunteer work, boards you sit on, leadership positions you have held, and prestigious memberships (skip *Who's Who* — everyone gets that.) List organizations that tell the recruiter good things about you — belonging to Mensa (*says you are very smart*), volunteering for Big Brothers & Big Sisters (*says that you care*), being a Guardian ad Litem (*you are civic minded*), volunteering for Habitat for Humanity (*you are actively engaged in improving your community*), etc. Don't list memberships unless you had or have a major role, title or quantifiable achievements.

+ **Citizenship and Work Status** If you are a US citizen, state it. If you are a foreign national or have a foreign-sounding name, indicate your immigration status, because otherwise your work status may be a barrier to consideration.

+ **Willingness to Relocate or Travel** If you are willing to relocate for the job, say so. If you are not able or willing to move, it's your choice to state it or not. You might leave it out, and then if they really want you, you might be able to negotiate a remote position, working from your home or a satellite office. If you are willing and able to travel for work, state it here.

+ **Unusual Skills or Hobbies** — List sports or unusual activities you participate in like marathons or Iron Man competitions, golf, tennis, racquetball, fly fishing — the possibilities are endless. Men love talking about sports, so add sports information and you may make a great impression if your interviewer is a fan or participant in the same sport. Highlight expertise in the arts — music, art, dance, etc. Mention extensive international travel — *"Exchange student in Norway for 8 months"* or *"Toured with Up With People to China and the Far East."* Showcase activities that portray you as an interesting, stimulating, curious and engaged person, the kind of person the interviewer would like to have as a friend or colleague.

Formatting Your Résumé

Think of your résumé like an advertising brochure or flier. It needs to be attractive, easy to read, visually interesting, and able to deliver your sales pitch efficiently before your "customer" moves on to the next brochure.

Your résumé should be attractively formatted, with a combination of bold texts, capitals, underlining and italics to guide the reader easily and quickly from section to section, highlighting the key information. Use white space to create emphasis and provide a visually soothing reading experience. If it's jumbled together and too busy, it will be harder to read and comprehend, and the reader will likely lose focus and interest.

It is often preferable to use a serif font like Times New Roman or Bookman. A serif font is one with the little squiggles at the top and bottom of the letter. It is the font used by newspapers, because it is easier on the eye than a non-serif font. I personally like to use Calibri, which is a narrow san-serif font, so the choice is up to you.

Use a 10, 11, or 12 font size; anything smaller will be too hard to read. Anything larger will look childish.

Due to your many years of experience, your résumé may run to two pages, but no longer. You might want to have two résumés — a concise one- to two-page summary résumé, as well as a detailed multi-page résumé with all those jobs you summarized in the Prior Experience section. Keep it for the interview, when you are asked for specifics of employment.

Proofread your résumé and have others do the same. You can't have one single error, typo, incorrect word usage, or poor grammar. Not one. Even one error may cause the reader to immediately quit reading and move on to the next candidate.

Preparing Your Résumé for Email Submission

When you are sending your résumé by email, make sure you do not label your attachment just "résumé." You can't imagine the number of résumés I receive without the candidate's name in the title of the file. If your résumé is titled "résumé," I will save it in my computer folder of submitted résumés and it will overwrite the last résumé from someone else that was titled *"résumé."* Then the next file labeled just *"résumé"* will overwrite your file and I will never be able to find your file if it's not labeled correctly.

Title your file with your first and last name, your desired job, and then *"résumé."* You can add year if you wish. The goal is to have it easily identifiable by the recipient if she wants to look it up in her files. Here are some naming examples:

+ DianeHuthRésumé-2018-VP Marketing
+ DianeHuth-Résumé-VP-Marketing
+ Diane_Huth_Résumé _2018_VPMarketing
+ Diane-Huth-Résumé -VPMktg-2018

No matter which naming format you choose, it should be crystal clear that the file is a résumé, whose résumé it is, what the desired position is, and when the file was submitted.

The same thing is true for the subject line of your email — make sure it is clear and includes your professional name along with the word *"résumé"* and possibly the desired position so it can be easily found in an email search.

Submitting Your Résumé For Online Submission

Unless your job posting instructions say differently, upload your résumé in both Word and PDF format. Your Word résumé can be scanned by all scanning programs, while some can't read a PDF. On the other hand, a PDF can be opened on any device, and saved to your Book folder on a phone or tablet for sharing and forwarding. Also, with a PDF, you can be confident that there won't be any file reading problem when received by email. If there is only room for one attachment, go with the Word document.

Make sure your résumé is loaded with the right keywords which match the job requirements that the search spiders will be looking for. Mention key words early in the document, especially in the Objective and Overview sections. Use multiple words to describe the same item to maximize search results — for example, "social media," "digital media," and "online media" might all describe the same activities and be used interchangeably and thus may be picked up separately by the search engines. Or you can list "accounting," "bookkeeping," "financial record keeping," "audit" and "Quick Books" to describe your accounting background. Mirror the job posting language to insert the identical key words in your résumé.

Don't Put Your Photo on Your Résumé

HR is mandated to eliminate potential discrimination based on race, ethnicity, age and appearance for government compliance reasons. They want an objective résumé that eliminates bias or discrimination. For this reason, about half of all recruiters will reject a résumé with a photo. However, you want them to like you and remember you over all other candidates. Unless your appearance would be detrimental to the selection process, my suggestion is to mail a résumé without a photo, but paper clip your business card (with your photo on it) to the résumé you are hand-delivering or mailing, so the interviewer will remember you. It's the same thing when you are applying for a job by cold calling the company. Whenever possible, mail a hardcopy of your résumé or even better, your "Broadcast Letter", with your business card clipped to it to stand out in the selection process.

Avoid Taboo Topics

- **Don't talk politics if at all possible.** Do not mention or include politics or political party affiliation, unless it is your paid job. Half of the people you interview with will be from the other party and they may think poorly of you for "bad judgment" for supporting a candidate or party they dislike.
- **Do not mention your religion.** If your volunteer or paid position includes work at your religious institution, just mention something like: *Lay Minister, church organist, head of church youth group, church choir member.* If the interviewer asks about it, of course feel free to discuss your religious affiliation at that time.
- **Don't say or write anything negative.** Never mention any employer or colleagues in a bad light, even if you left the employment against your will or quit over a bad situation. Prospective employers may see you as being petty, vindictive, and even untrustworthy, rather than confident and upbeat. They will assume that if they hire you, you may talk negatively or disclose confidential information about them. On too

many occasions I have seen firsthand where a disgruntled employee of a key competitor has come and "spilled the beans" about everything the company is doing. Our response was, *"Let's pick her brain for as long as we can, but we don't hire her. She can't be trusted."*

If you are an academic, with multiple advanced degrees and published papers, applying for a job teaching at a university or working at a research laboratory, you will probably want to use a CV — Curriculum Vitae — which contains all the gory details in many pages. Use Google to find the right formatting for a CV.

Seek Out Expert Opinion About Your Résumé

Once you think your résumé is perfect, ask objective third parties for their opinion, help and suggestions. You can't imagine the number of people who will read this book, or my e-book *BRAND YOU! Create Your Powerful Résumé*, and won't follow the instructions. Use these great tools and resources to fine tune your résumé:

- Show it to friends, counselors, mentors, even your grown children. They know you well and may think of strengths you overlooked. They can definitely help you proofread for typos and grammar!
- Ask for help at your local Job Services office; that's their business and they are great at it. Many non-profit associations also provide résumé and job search assistance such as Goodwill, AARP, Dress For Success®, and other career mentoring agencies.
- Call your university Alumni Office; they may offer help at no charge.
- Go to your favorite job-search website — Monster, Indeed, Ladders, etc. — and purchase résumé writing help. Expect to pay around $100–$200 to fine tune and format your résumé.
- Go to an independent résumé writing service. There are dozens more that you can find by a simple Google search. Again, expect to pay between $100 and $200 for a basic résumé rewrite or tweaking.

Make Sure Your Grammar and Spelling Are Perfect

Your résumé must be perfect in grammar and spelling, be pleasing to the reader's eye, and formatted to draw the reader's attention quickly to the important information.

It's not just me. 61% of recruiters and 43 % of hiring managers will discard your résumé because of a single typo or misspelling.

15

GATHER ALL YOUR JOB SEARCH TOOLS AND CREDENTIALS

Take time now to prepare and assemble all the tools and resources you will need for your job search. Don't wait until a potential employer asks you for references or letters of recommendation. Imagine how you'll come across if you say, *"My recommendations? I'll have to get back to you next week."*

Line Up Your Personal and Professional References

Every employer is going to want references, so be prepared with a list of both personal and professional references before an employer asks for them. They will include your current and former bosses, colleagues, vendors, customers, even colleagues from organizations you volunteer with. Select people who will write and say glowing things about you. Before you actively start your job search, call or talk with each of your mentors and ask if they will be willing to serve as a reference for you. Of course, the more impressive the title of the person, the more impressed your recruiter will be.

After they say "Yes" to acting as a reference for you, make sure you have their correct contact information, which includes their name, title, phone number, email and physical address. Create a nicely-formatted Word document with your contact information in the header or footer, and title it "References for John Doe." List each reference with contact information, and a brief one-sentence description of how you know or have worked with each person. Examples of suitable descriptions include:

- Served on the Board of the AMA chapter together from 2014-2016
- Direct supervisor at XYZ Corporation; can attest to my team work skills and attention to detail
- Ad agency account executive; worked together on the XYZ account

- Youth Ministry Pastor of XYZ church; worked together to host the summer Vacation Bible Camp in 2015
- Customer from 2010-2013; provided accounting services to his family-run landscaping business
- Business executive, longtime family friend; familiar with personal background and values

Take several copies of this list of references to your job interview. If the company seems interested, leave one copy with the HR director. Keep one handy to use in filling out the job application, which they will probably ask you to complete, even though they have your detailed résumé.

Save the file in both Word and PDF format, so you can forward it to your HR contacts with a follow-up email to thank them for your interview.

Get Glowing Letters of Recommendation

At the end of any job, ask for a letter of recommendation from your boss, his boss, the president of the company, vendors, customers, and anyone you have dealt with in a positive manner. Ask for a hard copy of the letter if possible, and then scan it and make copies. Never give away the original — keep it in your portfolio forever!

Many people will say *"I don't have the time to write a letter. Write a draft of what you want me to say and let me look at it."* So incredible as it may seem, you get to write your own recommendation letters! Put your modesty away and write rave reviews about yourself that are honest and realistic. Think *"If I were in her shoes, what qualities would she see in me? What would she say about me?"* and then you write that letter. Discuss successful projects, accomplishments, and the results achieved. Mention positive attributes and skills honed in the field that you want highlighted. The last line should always offer a phone number and email address for more information.

If you write a good and objective letter, the majority of the time, they will look at it, sign it and send it back.

Keep a packet of photocopied letters of recommendation, preferably in color and stapled together, which you can give to the interviewer after she has looked at the originals. These letters of recommendation are very, very valuable. Keep them in your hard copy portfolio. Mine from bosses I had thirty years ago are still in my portfolio, on letterhead, embossed and signed, available for inspection.

Master Your Elevator Pitch

Before you start networking or actively job searching, first develop a key tool, your Elevator Pitch.

Picture yourself in the elevator going to the 56th floor. A man you've always wanted to meet and work for is standing right there next to you. You have

just 30 seconds to make such a great impression that he'll gladly agree to an appointment or an interview. What are you going to say in those critical 30 seconds?

That's your Elevator Pitch — a 30-second ad that will tell him who you are, what you can do for him, provide proof that you can and will do it, and ask him for the interview.

Don't expect it to flow naturally. It's not something you can make up on the spot. If you're like 90% of us, you'd be tongue-tied. Instead, carefully craft a four- or five-sentence sales pitch, and wordsmith it until it's perfect. Practice until you can deliver it almost without thinking about it. It must feel and sound natural and unrehearsed and enthusiastic.

To put it in perspective, remind yourself that it only takes 30 seconds to get to the 56th floor, where your future job might be.

There Are Only 4 Key Elements of an Elevator Pitch:

Introduction

Introduce yourself audibly and memorably — *"Hi, Ellen, I'm Diane Huth. I'm the author of Brand YOU! to Land Your Dream Job."* Give her an audio cue if necessary so she'll remember your name.

What You Do and Can Do For Him

Tell him what you do for others or what you can do for him. *"I help job-seekers create a comprehensive and compelling self-branding program with a step-by-step guide so they can find and land their dream job."* Other examples might be:

- *"I work with small businesses to solve their legal issues before they become problems."*
- *"I help at-risk teenagers find their path in life and avoid drugs, crime and teen pregnancy."*
- *"I help businesses create brilliant advertising campaigns that achieve and surpass their sales goals."*
- *"I'm a marketing strategist and troubleshooter and I love solving branding problems so that you can increase your brand's preference and adoption by your target customers."*

Proof of Value

Next, you provide proof of value, to prove that you can do what you say you can do. *"Ellen, I have trained more than 2,000 graduating college students using my BRAND YOU! Program, and they have an impressive 88% hire rate within three months after taking my class."* Other examples might be:

- *"A consulting assignment I just completed with XYZ Bank repositioned their credit card products. New applications increased by 20% in just three months."*
- *"I've just completed 15 years at XYZ company where I led human resources and employee training programs for 800 employees in four different locations."*
- *"I've been on the Board of the SFA for the last seven years, and helped the organization grow by fifteen percent in the first four months."*

Call to Action

This is when you ask for what you want — the specific action you hope to achieve. *"Ellen, I'd like to come on your show and share tips on managing your social media presence so recruiters and employers can find and hire qualified viewers who are seeking jobs."*

Other calls to action might include:

- *"I would like to learn more about your company. Could you spare fifteen minutes in the next week so I could come by and learn more about your organization?"*

- *"Your company is just the kind of organization I've always wanted to work for. Could you join me for coffee to talk about your company and the job opportunities in your department?"*
- *"I have always wanted to work for your company. Could you introduce me to the hiring manager in the finance department?"*

Practice Your Elevator Pitch Until It Comes Naturally

After you draft your Elevator Pitch, practice it until it rolls off your tongue without thinking about it. When you meet Mr. Big in that elevator, fumbling in your pocket and saying, *"Oops, I may have misplaced my Elevator Pitch"* is not an option. In fact, your only option is to nail it right then and there. You need to practice it and memorize it until it feels natural.

Seriously, you should practice your Elevator Pitch at least 50 times before you need it. Pitch yourself in the bathroom mirror every morning and night. Practice while driving in the car or microwaving your morning cup of coffee — which will time it to exactly thirty seconds. Practice on family members, friends, colleagues, and when you're ready to give up, the family dog — she won't criticize you. Also practice shaking hands, smiling into a mirror, and giving your Elevator Pitch until it comes so naturally that you find yourself using it without thinking about it.

These 30 seconds can dramatically change your career path and your professional life.

Prepare Your Professional Portfolio

By now, your body of work accumulated over the years is no doubt extensive. How do you best present these key achievements to a potential employer?

Start with a Professional Hard Copy Portfolio

Collect samples of everything you have achieved during your career, plus projects that you legitimately worked on and supported, even if you were not solely responsible for the project execution.

If you haven't been saving samples of your work over the years, you may be able to find pieces on the internet. Start by googling the company, project, event or other program. Ask former or current colleagues what they have on hand. Or if you are still employed, go through the department archives to gather brochures, fliers, or other materials.

At the very least, download the company logo and images and create a one-page visual document that displays key achievements. PowerPoint is more visually-friendly than Word to tell a story about your contributions to your company goals.

Then create a powerful hard copy portfolio to showcase your work and skills. Add "show and tell" materials from a range of different jobs, volunteer work, professional associations, or spec work to demonstrate your skills.

Buy a nice presentation portfolio with oversized plastic sleeves to insert your samples — you may find one online or in an artist supply store. In the back, add your résumé, your references, copies of recommendation letters, copies of awards, prizes, certificates, scholarship award letters, college transcripts, newspaper and magazine clippings of a professional nature, and anything else that will showcase your skills and capabilities.

Arrange these nicely and artistically so they tell your story. If an interviewer asks, "Tell me about yourself," you can whip out your portfolio and say, "Let me show you what I am passionate about." Then let the portfolio speak for you. Tailor your narrative so it fits the job you are interviewing for.

Something magical happens during this process. You become excited and dynamic and passionate when you explain these interesting projects you have worked on, and that enthusiasm is contagious, they will think you are wonderful. This will, in turn, make you feel confident, credible and relaxed, which is not always easy in a high-stress interview.

It is a powerful way to engage with a potential hiring manager or prospective boss or colleague, because they may also be passionate about, or lose sleep over, the same things. Showcasing your professional accomplishments in this manner puts you firmly in the peer category, and allows you to have a conversation at a whole different level.

Create an Online Portfolio

Scan, photograph, or digitize all the samples and materials that go into your hard copy portfolio and use these to create a powerful online portfolio that you can easily share with a prospective employer through an email link or hyperlink on your résumé and LinkedIn page. For free online resources, check out Pathbrite and Issuu. LinkedIn recommends these five sites for online portfolios for creatives — Carbonmade, DROPR, Cargo Collective, Behance. net, and Coroflot.

You can create a virtual online portfolio by posting attachments and photos in your LinkedIn profile and in LinkedIn's SlideShare program. This can serve as a virtual online portfolio. Follow the same steps and post impressive samples of your work and achievements there so a recruiter can easily find them. If you post them on LinkedIn, consider a PowerPoint slide show that walks viewers step-by-step though your career trajectory with these rich visuals to give them a good flavor of your accomplishments and skills.

Having an online portfolio also helps subtly neutralize an employer's concerns about your technology skills.

SO WHAT DO YOU REALLY WANT TO DO?

If you're reading this book, it probably means you want to find a job — *now* . . . or as soon as possible The reasons can vary, but the immediacy may not. You may be:

- Frustrated and fearful that your career has hopelessly stalled, and you are desperate to get it going — somehow;
- Looking for a raise, a promotion or a better or more meaningful job;
- Tired of working long hours at no extra pay to keep your current job;
- Recently unemployed and looking to get back to work to pay bills and get medical insurance;
- Out of the work force for months, years or even decades, caring for family members, raising your own family, or traveling the world;
- One of the alarmingly large number of long-term unemployed who just gave up;
- Just plain bored, after years or decades in the same job, and the thought of going to work knots your stomach and gives you the urge to run away from everything including the responsibility of being an adult;
- Retired too early and miss the stimulation of your job and colleagues;
- All your friends are working and you feel left out;
- Fearful that retirement funds will run out;
- Hate your boss or industry or company.

All of these and others are valid reasons to embark on a job search mission. What matters is that *you* crave a change.

Working with hundreds of job seekers over decades, I've learned the most important step is always the same: Ask yourself, "*What is it that I really want to do?*" It is probably very different from your career goals from 10, 20, 30 or more years ago.

That's because along with changes in the job, the industry and the market, *you* have changed dramatically. You have grown professionally and personally. Everything else has changed along with you: your family, your financial situation, your skills portfolio, perhaps your health or any of a thousand different things have shifted over time.

So before you make any big decisions, accept a job, or fill out the next round of online job applications, step back and figure out how much money you *need* to earn, how much you *want* to earn, and the trade-offs between them.

16

REVISE YOUR EARNINGS EXPECTATIONS

As you evaluate your employment options, it is important to rethink your salary expectations. How much do you *want* to earn? How much do you *need* to earn? They are generally not the same.

We all have salary numbers that we aspire to earn — $50,000, $75,000, $100,000 or more annually. At those levels of income, you are probably a salaried employee, with a weekly, bi-weekly, or monthly paycheck. Your paycheck is further reduced with lots of withholding for taxes, Social Security, Medicare, and insurance premiums — a minimum of 10% for federal government deductions, and often up to 20% of your overall pay with group benefit contributions and insurance premiums.

You probably end up having your paycheck automatically deposited into your bank account, so you may not realize exactly how much you earn on an hourly basis, and what it takes to replace that income.

I have never met anyone who earned a $100,000 salary and who worked less than 60 to 70 hours a week, and often up to 80 hours weekly. I know I have never worked less than 70 or 80 hours a week, whether employed by Corporate America or start up ventures.

How Much Do You Need to Earn on An Hourly Basis?

When you break down those big salaries on an hourly basis, add in vacation and sick leave, and all the overtime you work, the numbers may surprise you.

A $100,000 salary comes out to just $24.04 per hour based on an 80-hour week, or $32.05 if you can get away with just 60 hours a week.

Likewise, a person making $75,000 annually earns from $20.60 to $28.80 per hour, depending on whether she works 50 to 70 hours a week.

And someone earning $50,000 per year makes between $16.03 and $24.04 hourly, working even fewer hours weekly.

How Much Do You Earn Hourly?				
Annual Salary	Montly Salary	Weekly Salary	# Hours Worked	Hourly Earnings
$100,000	$8,333	$1,923	80	$24.04
			70	$27.47
			60	$32.05
$75,000	$6,250	$1,442.31	70	$20.60
			60	$24.04
			50	$28.85
$50,000	$4,166.67	$961.54	60	$16.03
			50	$19.23
			40	$24.04

Of course, your salary comes with fringe benefits and health insurance which ups the equivalent pay. But it also comes with lots of expenses, including the cost of commuting, lunch out, maintaining a professional wardrobe, and more.

As you look at your desired job and salary, you might want to consider trade-offs between the salary and the expenses and time commitment the job entails.

Commuting Costs

It is estimated that it costs you around $1,000 per year per mile to commute to work, in time and expense, according to an article *The True Cost of Commuting* posted by Mr. Mustache on *Lifehacker.com*.

So if you have a 20-mile commute each way, it costs you $20,000 per year in minimum salary and auto expenses. He recommends living near work and bicycling to the job instead. All of a sudden, working at home and having a home office starts sounding really attractive.

Home Office Deductions

If you work out of a bona fide home office, you may be able to deduct a substantial amount of home office expenses to reduce your taxable income, which will save you thousands in taxes. If you run your own business out of your home, this deduction continues. But the 2017 tax law change has made it more difficult for company employees to deduct home office expenses. Check out the instructions on IRS Form 8829 for updated information starting in 2018.

Medical Expense Coverage for Older Workers

The older you are, the more you pay for medical insurance. A couple of years ago, workers at 60 were charged five to six times more than younger employees, and premiums were $1,000 per month or more.

The Affordable Care Act (Obamacare) capped premiums for older workers at three times higher than the youngest covered adult at age 21. However, new legislation allows insurers to charge seniors five times more for premiums. Low-cost access to medical services is also long gone, until you get Medicare. Deductibles and co-pays are often $5,000 or $10,000 or more annually, which again can bankrupt an unemployed or budget-limited job seeker even with insurance.

More than eight years ago, I paid $850 per month in COBRA premiums! They have skyrocketed since then, and are very likely to continue to increase.

If you are currently unemployed, consider taking a much lower-level job than you had previously considered, or take a job you don't love if you don't find other options, if it at least gives you access to affordable health insurance subsidized by a company. According to Nicole Felan and Marci Martin in an article in *Business News Daily*, some firms in industries with chronically-high turnover offer group medical insurance to their part-time workers as a recruiting and retention tool: Starbucks, Lowes, REI, Caribou Coffee, UPS and McDonalds.

By moving from no insurance, COBRA or an expensive or high-deductible plan to group medical coverage through a lower level job, you can actually increase your equivalent earnings by up to $5.00 per hour.

Anyone with work skills and experience can get an entry-level job at a call center earning $12–$15 per hour, plus bonuses and commissions on occasion. Add in the $5 per hour medical insurance benefit, and now you are looking at hourly compensation approaching $17–$20 per hour — an hourly rate similar to that of a worker earning $75,000 per year and working 70 hours a week. If you want a higher salary, simply offer to work overtime to make additional compensation. Even better would be to find a work at home job and you may get some home office deductions while saving the commute cost!

Of course, you want a great professional level job with a great salary and benefits. Everyone does. Hold on to it if you can find one. But open your mind to different options if you really want a job fast.

Take a realistic look at your job and the number of hours you have dedicated to it, then look at your current or prior salary and the true hourly rate you earn (or earned) in perspective. It may end up opening new doors and work opportunities you would never have considered before. You might be able to actually enjoy the weekend and evenings at home with your family. It would allow you to stop thinking or worrying about the job or checking emails and dashing to your computer whenever something "urgent" pops up that requires your attention 24/7. That's the beauty of an hourly job — you leave it behind when you leave the office at night. Maybe that's not such an awful trade off after all.

17

THE CONCEPT OF "RETIREMENT" HAS CHANGED

Several decades ago, you worked for 30 years, and then got a gold watch, a livable pension, and you "retired." You left the workplace, resettled in Florida, and played golf or bridge all day long until you died.

According to the dictionary, retirement means withdrawing, retreating, and falling back. It is synonymous with failure, defeat, and giving up. Who wants to do that?

We know all about retirement — it's driven home by those commercials touting companies that want to help you manage your investments and plan for your future — for a fee. There supposedly are hoards of attractive, trim and fit men and women with silver streaks in their perfectly coiffed hair, in loving relationships, holding hands while they walk on a beach outside their delightful dream cottage. That is what Corporate America is selling us.

Not one of them is overweight, wrinkled, bald, wears glasses, has bags under her eyes, is widowed, suffers from diabetes or limps from bad knees or flat feet.

If we live to the predicted mid-80's life expectancy or longer, we should have very different expectations which reflect today's reality. We might:

* Have to work well into our 70's to bridge the financial gap;
* Want to work because we are healthy, intelligent, have enjoyed interesting careers, like feeling valued and productive and giving back to the world;
* Don't like being bored;
* Want to create a legacy or leave the world a better place.

Regardless of the reasons, most of us want to remain productive and feel worthwhile, especially as we grow older. We want and need to support ourselves and our loved ones beyond the meager funds we receive from Social Security each month.

Dozens of great books are readily available that give you valuable investment advice, wonderful retirement planning strategies, teach you to live frugally, or help you figure out how and where to travel in your golden years.

I won't go into those topics in this book. I will focus on the goal of finding productive, profitable and meaningful employment.

But that work may be very different from what you've done in the past or ever imagined doing. You may hop back into the Corporate America 80-hour-a-week whirlwind. You may want or need to stay in your current position as long as you can get to work every day.

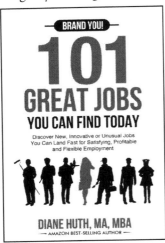

Alternately, you may opt to work part time, flex time, share a job with a colleague, work from your home office, consult, do gig assignments, or quit the rat race and become a bartender at a beach bar. You may decide to buy an ongoing business or start your own, invest in a franchise, or open a real estate or insurance sales office. Or you might just say, "Let the young hot shots worry about everything," and become an Uber, Lyft or school bus driver (schools pay medical insurance!) Perhaps you will choose to go to a tech school to get your CNA certification to become a caregiver, or teach English online while living on a white sandy beach in Mexico. (Note a trend here about retiring on white sandy beaches? It's what I fantasize about!) I explore all these options, and many more, in the companion book *101 Great Jobs You Can Find Today*.

With that said, before you take any drastic steps, try to figure out what you really *want* to do for productive work today.

If you don't have a dream, you'll never have a dream come true.

Here are three different exercises to help you find out what your dream job is at this point of your life, so you have a chance of achieving it.

The first is quick and easy, the second, more difficult, and the last, life-changing.

18

WHAT ARE YOUR PERSONAL PASSIONS?

This is an easy one to get you started. It probably won't disrupt your world, but should get you started thinking about where you are headed, and why.

Before you seriously embark on your job search, you need to know what you want in a job, and why. If you plan to stay in your current career because you love what you do, you can skip this section.

However, if you are considering changing careers, or are confused about what you ought to do, work through this quick exercise to start a serious examination of your career options.

Create Your Professional Passion Matrix

My colleague and mentor John Highland uses what I call the Professional Passion Matrix to help figure out the right career path for job candidates and employees. He developed this process when he was a senior consultant at McKinsey, a leading consulting firm, and has used it ever since when interviewing job candidates.

Ask yourself 4 questions — right now — and write down the answers:

1. What do you do BEST?

_____

_____

2. What do you LOVE to do?

_____

_____

3. What are your key WEAKNESSES?

_____

_____

4. What do you HATE to do?

_____

_____

Making Sense of the Answers

1. **What you do BEST** is what you should be doing because it is your key strength. It is the tangible set of skills you offer your employer. This is the easiest job to find right now because you can demonstrate expertise and mastery. It should pay your bills today.

2. **What you LOVE to do** is your future. It's where you should strive to be long term. Look for jobs that allow you to grow into that dream job. Work on gaining the skills and experience to move into that position as soon as possible. Take online courses, go back to school, study for a certification, join a trade association, or network with other professionals in the field.

3. **Your WEAKNESSES** are what may keep you from attaining your goal. First, determine whether or not these are critical to success in your field and future career. Focus on more relevant weaknesses first. For example, if you are an accountant, and public speaking is your weakness, it probably is not a deal breaker. However, if you work in marketing or sales, it may be detrimental to your success. If you determine that these weaknesses *are* critical to your success, you need to take action immediately to improve your skills, and hopefully to gain expertise in the field. Hire a tutor, sign up for classes, hire a life coach, take online courses, go to a workshop or seminar, and then practice the skill set until you reach an acceptable level. In the case of the person seeking a marketing job, in order

to feel self confident, that might mean joining Toastmasters for public speaking experience, taking an acting or debate class and reading books on public speaking techniques.

4. **Avoid doing what you HATE.** There is no reason to make yourself miserable by taking a job that you will hate every day. In addition, you will probably do poorly at any job you really hate. You will be a failure at that job and hate it even more. For example, I really hate cold calling and direct sales, especially telephone sales. It gives me a knot in my stomach and makes me nervous, anxious and irritable. So I avoid getting around to making those awful sales calls until it's the end of the day and too late to do anything. Sometimes I'll just make busywork to avoid making the calls at all. I don't do it well, and I am miserable. It's not the right job for me. Other people love direct sales, relish the challenge, wake up excited to get to work to start calling on new customers. That's the right job for them. So find a job you really enjoy; you will be happier. And your company will be more successful and profitable.

The Personal Passions Matrix

What do you do BEST? This is what you should be doing now.	What do you LOVE to do? This is your future.
What are your key WEAKNESSES? Work to master these skills.	What do you HATE to do? Avoid this at all costs.

Find Your Professional Passion Before Embarking on Your Job Search

Take the time now to find the right career path *for you*. If you are considering a new career or job in a field that is different from what you are currently doing, consider:

- Working with a career coach or counselor if possible;
- Finding out what vocational testing and coaching is available for free from your state unemployment or job services office to help you figure out your skills and aptitudes;
- Talking with people in the new field to make sure the work fits your interests and temperament;
- Finding someone in that field and ask for half an hour of their time so you can ask detailed questions about the realities of the job and discuss pros and cons. I suggest offering to buy them coffee after work or treating for a working lunch near their office;
- Shadowing someone at work for a day to directly experience the realities of the job; (this might require HR's permission at a large company but should be feasible at a smaller company);
- Offering to volunteer for a week or so to see how the job feels — consider it an unpaid internship or "returnship." In the process, you may make yourself so valuable they hire you to stay on permanently.

19

FIGURE OUT YOUR LIFESTYLE CHANGES AS YOU AGE

We all expect to live a long, full, rich life. I haven't heard anyone say, "I'm planning to die at 67, so I will work until 65 and retire to a nursing home." But many of us probably haven't charted out what we expect our life to look like at age 60, 65, 70, 75, 80, 85 — which is the average life expectancy today. Many of us may have a good chance of living longer, into our late 80s or even our 90s.

Now is the time to really envision what you want or expect your life will look like at each of the five-year benchmarks in front of you.

This is a very difficult task.

We all see ourselves in our current state of health, fitness and affluence, and we expect we will continue that way until we die. But that isn't really realistic.

I've been caring for my mom with Alzheimer's Disease, now at age 95, which I never anticipated. She was always the sharpest, smartest, most clever and active person I knew. Now she is a child-like shell of her former self, withering away physically, living in a mind ravaged by dementia.

Decline and infirmity are part of the natural progression of life and one of the realities we will need to deal with, whether we plan for it or not. We all need to consider the impact of our health and wellness on our future lives now while we can.

Are you married and in a relationship? What would happen financially and emotionally if your spouse becomes ill, or dies? How will that impact your plans and your financial and physical ability to care for yourself and your home?

To do this task justice, go to *www.BrandYouGuide.com/AgingWorksheet* and download it. But for now, try to think through the key topics and options. Write down how you expect to be at each five-year mark until the 90s or later.

Expected Health Status

+ Excellent — fully active and mobile, youthful
+ Very Good — active and mobile
+ Good — some activity, some mobility challenges
+ Fair — not in great health, inactive, limited mobility
+ Poor — inactive, wheelchair bound

Where Do You Plan to Live?

+ Current city or town
+ Move to a retirement location
+ Move to live near kids or grandkids
+ Move to live near someone else
+ Other or unknown

Housing Needs

+ Own current stand-alone home
+ Move to a different stand-alone home
+ Apartment or townhome with minimal upkeep
+ Live with children or other family members
+ Independent living community
+ Assisted living community
+ Nursing home

Financial Sustainability — Monthly - Calculate for You + Spouse

+ Social Security anticipated earnings
+ Pension anticipated earnings
+ Annuity anticipated earnings
+ Other monthly passive earnings

   = Total Expected Monthly Retirement Earnings
   − Expected Monthly Expenses
   = Amount You Need to Earn Monthly

Work Goals

+ Work full time in current field
+ Work half time in current field
+ Work sporadically in any field

+ Work in a low-stress job
+ Volunteer for unpaid work
+ Not work or volunteer at all

Incremental Earnings Goals

+ $100,000 annually
+ $75,000 annually
+ $50,000 annually
+ $25,000 annually
+ Work to augment Social Security or pension
+ Secure, no need to earn more money

Many valid options are available, so really weigh your current circumstances with your lifestyle aspirations as you age. There is no right or wrong choice, just what is right for you right now.

Discuss your finances with a financial or legal advisor. I'm not one, but I can tell you with 100% confidence that today is the time to plan how you want to live tomorrow and into the future.

20

IF YOU WIN THE LOTTERY TODAY...

Plan to spend at least half an hour with this exercise; an hour or more if you can spare it. It may change your life.

Grab several sheets of clean paper, and a pen or pencil. Then find a quiet place, get comfortable, close your eyes, and go on an imaginary trip with me.

Imagine that this week you bought a lottery ticket when you filled up the gas tank, and it's in your wallet. Pull it out of your wallet, hold it in your hands, look at the numbers on the third row, and realize that you have just WON!

Visualize yourself going online to make sure that your numbers really are winners. The TV announcer wasn't mistaken.

See yourself jumping for joy, hugging everyone around you, whooping with excitement, then yell, *"I won! I'm a millionaire! I'm rich."*

That's right. You just won 10 million dollars! That's enough to do anything you want for the rest of your life (within reason), and it's not so much that you have to spend all your time actively managing it. You're not Mark Cuban-wealthy. You can't go out and buy a football franchise or invest millions every week in great Shark Tank ideas. But you can live very comfortably and take care of the people you love pretty much forever.

Now, plan step-by-step exactly what you will do the day it sinks in that you never have to worry about money again.

Picture yourself telling your spouse and kids and your parents. They scream with excitement and joy and hug you and each other. See and feel the tears of joy as you realize that everyone you care about can be taken care of. Never again will you stress about making the mortgage or the tuition payments.

What will you do about work? Will you call up your boss and resign on the spot? Or will you ask for a leave of absence while you work out all the life changes ahead of you? Will you plan to go back to work on Monday just like you have every Monday for years? Or will you be like the boy who mowed my lawn when I lived in Miami? His parents won $360 million in the lottery, and I never saw or heard from him or his family again!

Of course, you'll need a financial advisor right away, to plan ways that you can enjoy your windfall without burning through it. This will ensure that you won't run out of money before you die. Better yet, plan to provide a nest egg for your kids and grandkids. You will no doubt update wills, set up trust accounts and college savings accounts, investing wisely so every month you'll have a steady stream of income that provides enough to do whatever you want.

Then pamper yourself! Take a substantial amount — maybe half a million dollars — to fulfill your fondest dreams and those of your loved ones.

Make a list of all the people you will give cash to. Perhaps you will want to give $50,000 to each of your kids or grandkids for a down payment on their first home, buy a prepaid college plan or a 529 plan for their college educations, or give $10,000 to a long-time friend who works so hard and is struggling under crushing credit card debt.

Next, pay off all your debts. Feel the freedom as you write those checks to pay off every single credit card you owe. Then see yourself cutting up most of the credit cards — you will never need them again. Get a black AMEX card with your newfound wealth! Go to your bank, and with a flourish, hand them a check to pay off your mortgage in full. Maybe have a mortgage deed burning party with your friends! Pay off other debts too: car loans (or trade in your old car and buy a new one — in cash), personal loans or promissory notes. Feel the weight lift off your shoulders — isn't it fabulous?

You'll still have enough to make a generous donation to your church or temple, and to a bunch of your favorite charities. Endow a chair at your alma mater. What feels better than taking care of the people you care about? Sit back and bask in the joy of the moment.

Wow, that was a busy first week!

Next, indulge yourself. You deserve it! If you've always dreamed of a "toy" or experience that was out of your reach, say a Tesla, handmade Italian shoes, a trip to Thailand, or a designer suit...go for it — with cash. Then savor rubbing the hand-tooled leather of the car seats, or the fabric of your new suit. For my female readers, nothing will feel better than a cut, color, and styling at a top salon.

Next, buy gifts for everyone you love. That diamond ring you've promised your wife all those years. The motorcycle your husband has dreamt about forever. A fancy new top-of-the-line Apple computer for your graphic designer son or granddaughter...you get the picture.

It will be another busy week or two to get all this done. Pat yourself on the back, bring in your home masseuse, and take a breather.

Next, think about your home — and where you really want to live. If you aren't tied to your current city for jobs, where would you choose to live? Perhaps a beautiful home overlooking the Caribbean? Or a New England lake house you've always dreamed about? Maybe life in a French cottage in Provence has more appeal. So many choices! Real estate purchases and sales take lots of thought, time and effort because where you live affects every aspect of your life. Talk with other family members. This should take another one to possibly three months.

Now celebrate! Go on that Mediterranean cruise you've always talked about with your whole family. At the end of the tour, rent a huge villa overlooking the Amalfi coast for another two weeks.

By month five or six, you may have sold your house and bought a new one, so set about decorating your dream home just the way you want it. Moving takes a while, despite getting rid of so much because you have new furnishings. Another three or four weeks are gobbled up.

Finally you're in your beautifully-decorated new home. Throw a house-warming party and invite all your friends. With so much spare time now, you can cook beautiful meals with your gorgeous new outdoor kitchen on the patio overlooking a breathtaking vista. Without work occupying your days, you can go golfing several times a week if you wish, or go to the spa, get a massage every week. Or do whatever you wish to do as often as you want.

Spend a week or two bumming around town, visiting friends, going to museums or the zoo or the planetarium, places you never had time to visit when you were working so hard. Have lunch at fancy restaurants with friends who can take time off from work long enough to join you. Go shopping any time you like and buy anything that strikes your fancy.

Next, start working on you. Join a health club and start working out at least three times a week. Get a makeover — hair, make-up, facial, nails, the works. Buy a new wardrobe. Get your teeth bleached. Liberate yourself from glasses with expensive lenses implanted during cataract surgery. Hire a housekeeper so you never have to scrub dirty floors again — your new manicure deserves it.

Just imagine, all this has taken you six months, maybe seven or eight months or more if there were any delays with the real estate transactions.

Now think about next week. What will you do next week? Plan it out day by day. More shopping….lunches out…..golf with favorite buddies? Where will you go out for dinner? Is there a play in town you want to see — or a new movie? Go and see them. Start re-reading all the books by your favorite author — you've finally got the time.

And what will you do the following week. What will you do then....and the week after that?

Congratulations — you envisioned a future with no day-to-day responsibilities or financial worries and all the time in the world to do whatever you want. Do you feel bored or energized? Will you write the book you wanted to, but didn't have time? Sign up for interesting classes at the library? What will you do to help advance the causes you are passionate about, whether helping the homeless, fighting against injustice, bullying or childhood obesity? Of course, a donation is always welcome. But what will you do with your time, effort, energy and creativity? Volunteer for a cause? Start a new charity to fight for a better outcome? Will you do something to make a difference in the world?

Visualize yourself now. You've paid off your bills, invested money so you have enough not just to live on but to really enjoy, taken care of your family financially, traveled extensively and treated those you care about to memorable adventures. You've gifted yourself and loved ones with long-lusted-after luxuries. You live in the home of your dreams, drive a new car you love, wear beautiful clothes, and look and feel great. It's been a very busy six or eight months.

What will the next six months hold, and the six months after that?

We are human beings with purpose. As Maslow explained with his hierarchy of needs, we focus on the most urgent and dire needs first — food, shelter, safety, then move up to love and belonging. As those needs are met, we are able to engage in higher-level needs of self-esteem, beauty, knowledge, and eventually self-actualization and transcendence.

Maslow's Hierarchy of Needs

Your lottery luck has enabled you to satisfy your lower-level needs, so you can now dedicate your energies to higher level goals.

Write down on the paper what you would do with your time and energy and talents if money were never an issue again.

This task may be hard or easy.

Have you always loved animals and have rallied against the cruelty of traditional shelters that euthanize unadoptable pets? Your choice may be easy — establish a no-kill shelter in your town, and lobby politicians to enact no-kill laws throughout the state or country.

Perhaps you love ballet. Take ballet classes and become a prima ballerina — at your age! Why not? Or if that isn't a possibility, you can underwrite the annual performance of great ballets in your city by creating a non-profit organization that supports ballet. It might include a ballet school for small children, and the opportunity to perform on stage with hundreds of aspiring dancers.

Maybe your passion is hunting. Now you can buy the hunting cabin and lease you've always wanted and become a hunting guide. Imagine — you can go hunting every day you want!

Have you invented a product that you believe will make people's lives easier or happier, but never brought it to market? Now is the time. You can afford plenty of help with marketing, prototypes, startup, exporting, and the rest to help you manufacture and sell your invention, so go for it!

You think women's abuse and foster care in this country are a national disgrace? Set up an organization to provide quality homes for unwed mothers, an emergency shelter for abused women and their children, or fund adoptions to middle class parents that can't afford $20,000 to adopt a baby from a developing country. Or facilitate the adoption process in our own foster system.

Find your dream, visualize it, make it as tangible in your mind and heart as possible. See it, touch it, feel it, hold it. Now write down exactly what it is that you want to dedicate your unlimited time and attention to creating or achieving.

Why Wait?

If you've found your passion, why wait until you win the lottery to start making it happen? Start today.

Would you live in a different place if money were not an issue? If you need to work for your financial survival, look for a job in the field or market that will allow you achieve your goal. Start exploring those options and land your next job in your ideal location.

Have you always wanted to write a book? Get started now. All it takes is to sit down and not get up until you have written 1,000 words every day. There are many great programs that will help you to turn that dream a reality.

If ballet is your passion, apply for jobs at performing arts centers, or dance studios, or pitch the Parks and Recreation Department to hire you to establish summer or year-around performing dance classes at local recreation centers.

Are you the animal lover? Get a paying job at a shelter or humane society. If paying jobs aren't available, become a volunteer now and work your way into a position when it opens up.

Think of your time as a volunteer or even a paid employee as OJT (On the Job Training). Use those skills, insights and contacts to enable you to set up your own program when the timing is right. Or jump in now, start small, and with each successful step, share your vision with more and more people.

Sadly, you didn't win 10 million dollars (and neither did I.) You don't have your cottage in France (yet), or your Tesla (yet) or your mortgage and credit cards paid off (yet.) But hopefully, you do have a vision of your passions, what really matters to you, and how to invest your time, energy, skills and talents to enrich your life long term.

With your vision firmly in place, you can use work to achieve it. One option is to continue at your current or planned job, unrelated to your dream, until you actually retire with a pension or Social Security check, and then start focusing on what makes you happy. The other is to start pursuing work now that will bring you closer to achieving your long-term goal. Either way, take concrete steps in the right direction that lead you to living life with passion.

Don't wait until you win the lottery to do what you're passionate about. Find your dream, visualize it, make it tangible in your mind and heart as soon as possible. See it, touch it, feel it, hold it. Even if you need a job for financial survival, start by working in the field or market that will launch you toward achieving your goal.

SECTION 5

MAKE FINANCIAL AND LIFESTYLE CHOICES NOW

Review your finances, and ask yourself, *"If I were to become suddenly unemployed, could I comfortably maintain my current lifestyle?"* If you have a great pension or substantial savings to last you well into your late 80s or 90s (at least two million dollars in savings and investments, which few people have), you have the luxury of time to plan for your future and take proactive steps to ensure your long-term financial well-being.

If not, like the rest of us, you could be one pink slip away from joining the ranks of the unemployed, based not on your own merits, but on a multitude of conditions beyond your control — a younger boss who doesn't value your experience, a new CEO who changes direction or brings in his own trusted team, the closure of your office or division, mandatory RIFs (reduction in force), a business downturn, a merger or acquisition, a change in governmental regulations, or unexpected legal actions that affect your company.

Any of these and many other situations could leave you unemployed. The sudden halt of cash flow could be devastating unless you've prepared in advance.

Professional financial planners, credible online resources, non-profit credit counseling services, even friends and neighbors may give you sound advice. Always be cautious, however, especially if any "freelance advisor" wants banking or any other personal information. Desperate boomers are, sadly, prime prey for scam artists, especially women.

Some of the options below may insulate you from a cash calamity and prepare you for your future joy-filled lifestyle.

21

BECOME FRUGAL AT FIFTY

To help you survive short term and prosper long term, the first step is to reorganize your thinking and finances. If the kids are grown and you are contemplating retirement or a dramatic lifestyle change, you have complete control over the simplest way to free up cash: spend less! Here are some basics to consider today:

The ABCs of Saving More

+ Take advantage of all your tax-deferred savings options. Contribute the maximum amount to your IRA or 401K. Consider setting up any other available tax-deferred income plan — SEP, Solo IRA, etc. A self-directed IRA can be used to invest in closed businesses, investment real estate and other private business ventures;
+ Reduce expenses however you can, and put as much as possible into savings accounts;
+ Keep enough in liquid assets to cover six months of expenses in case of an unexpected reduction in income.

Pre-pay Expenses

Pre-pay as many future expenses as possible including:
+ A Health Savings Account, which can roll over year after year so the money is never lost;
+ State prepaid college funds or pre-tax federal 529 accounts for kids and grandkids;
+ Whole-life policies or annuities to help make future income more predictable and to pass assets tax-free to your heirs (consult your financial advisor);
+ Prepaid cremation or funeral plan.

Eliminate Debt

Make a concerted effort to pay off all credit cards so you can live debt free. If you have high-interest rate credit cards charged to the maximum, you will probably be paying around 24% interest. A $25,000 debt will incur interest of $500 per month, plus another $100 or $200 of principal, which is as much as many people earn in Social Security each month. A catastrophic illness or devastating job loss could rack up credit card debts like this in a relatively short time.

There are ways to reduce the interest rates, including taking a home equity line of credit if you own your own home.

Some credit cards will offer you free transfers with a new high-limit card and 0% interest for the first year. You can move highest-interest balances to the new cards, paying the minimum due, and paying off other high interest cards first. Carefully manage debt and interest rates on cards to save money, which you can then use to pay off debts.

Many unemployed or fixed-income baby boomers are too far in debt to be able to pay off such a staggering debt within a reasonable period of time. In this case, you may want to consider debt counseling, consolidation, or settlement. Search for a non-profit organization online in your area, possibly affiliated with your city, county or state government's consumer services. Your local United Way organization might also refer you to a reputable non-profit credit counseling service that can help you navigate the various options.

As a last resort, you might consider bankruptcy. Fixed income seniors with high debts can often weather a bankruptcy easier than younger individuals, since generally your home, modest car, IRAs and 401Ks, Social Security, Veterans benefits, and pensions are exempt from consideration or judgment. If you consult with a bankruptcy attorney, he will almost certainly recommend bankruptcy as the solution, which may or may not be your best option. This is a very important decision, so make sure you do a great deal of research and consult with several different non-profit credit counselors before taking any action.

Become Flexible, Mobile and Agile

At this point in your life, flexibility and mobility may be key to living a vibrant, satisfying life. If your kids no longer live with you, now may be the time to become more mobile and responsive. What will you do if one of your parents becomes ill and you need to care for them for months or even years in a different city or state? Will you be tied down and unable to react if your son is transferred out of state, and your grandchildren, whom you care for every afternoon, are suddenly thousands of miles away? If you, your spouse or a family member suffers a medical crisis, will you be prepared to move quickly to get treatment at an out-of-state facility? Your company may downsize and offer you a transfer to another city. What do you do — move for the job, or stay for the house?

Look for ways to become more flexible and mobile as you age and face myriad career and personal shifts that may be outside of your control. This may be the time to become agile and ready to react quickly if and when the need arises.

22

HOME SWEET HOME...OR IS IT?

Why wait for the unexpected to happen before protecting yourself, when it might be too late? Regardless of your employment situation, this may be this time to change your lifestyle and living arrangements to become more agile and ready for unexpected changes. A good way to free up cash is to sell the home where you raised your family. Moving into a smaller one-story home or low maintenance townhouse may better suit your empty nester lifestyle and health and mobility issues as you age.

I never expected I would tear the meniscus in my knee in my mid 50s and be confined to a wheel chair for several weeks while bouncing between doctors, labs and imaging centers before surgery. I couldn't climb the stairs to my bedroom and office. My home wasn't wheelchair-friendly even on the first story — just getting to the living and dining room from the family room and kitchen was a huge challenge due to just three steps. After that, I swore I would never live in a two-story home again. If you or a family member experiences an unexpected health or mobility problem, is your home ready?

Do some soul-searching now. If you can move to a smaller home and cut your living expenses in half, you'll take tons of pressure off your shoulders. Check out these suggestions for building an even bigger financial cushion by making changes in your home today:

Share a Home With Family Members

My friend Cheryl, a divorced mom with a grown daughter, works fulltime as a medical services sales rep. She often spends evenings and weekends caring for her grandbaby. Cheryl struggled for decades to maintain her lovely three bedroom empty-nest home on one salary — hers. She and her daughter came up with a brilliant solution — sell their two smaller three-bedroom houses and build a larger two-story home customized to their multi-generational lifestyle, including two big living areas. The five-bedroom house is split; her daughter and husband have the downstairs master suite. Cheryl converted two small bedrooms upstairs into her bedroom with a huge walk in closet, and transformed the large upstairs landing area into her living room. She kept just enough furniture and treasures to make the new space feel like home. When her house sold, she contributed $60,000 to the new mortgage and banked the rest of her equity. She now enjoys a rent-free, comfortable life at home *and* has a financial safety net. Her monthly contribution for utilities is $100. For the first time in more than a decade, she doesn't worry about making the mortgage payment, hauling the trash to the curb, or mowing the lawn. Instead, she's traveling, visiting friends on weekends, and enjoying the deepest financial cushion she's had in more than 20 years.

This in an attractive option, but a word of caution — if you choose an arrangement like this, prepare a written agreement that fully details what happens if contingencies occur that change the structure of the initial deal. If her daughter decides to sell the house, does Cheryl get back her $60,000? If yes, with accrued interest or appreciation? If Cheryl meets Mr. Right and moves out, can she get her money back? The better the agreement is thought through and negotiated up front, the easier it will be for all parties to move on if they have a change of heart. Detail what you agreed to in writing, then have a lawyer review it and create a contract in "legalese." Make sure all parties sign the agreement. Put one copy in your safety box; keep others on-hand for guidance.

If you haven't already read Robert Kiyosaki's best-selling book *Rich Dad, Poor Dad*, get it now and read it cover to cover. If you've read it before, re-read it in light of your current situation. He emphasizes that anything you pay for (like a mortgage) is a liability, and to focus instead on assets such as rental property that spins off cash. If you look at your home from a liability perspective and realize just how heavy a liability it is, it might be easier to let it go. But if your mortgage is paid off on a house that's too big for you, think of the passive income from rentals, businesses, and investments you could be making if you choose to sell or repurpose it!

You might decide to cash out of the real estate market and rent or buy a smaller home, freeing up your capital to invest in liquid assets or in sources of passive income. Perhaps it's time to divest yourself of your summer cabin, the boat at the lake, and other "assets" which cost you money, and invest the proceeds to increase your savings or passive income. If you want to take a vacation at the lake, by all means do so, and rent a cabin from Home Away or Airbnb. You don't need to do without that family vacation — just do it in a way that doesn't tie up your income-generating assets. If you need to move for work or family reasons, it won't matter where your source of passive income is located.

Turn Your Home Into a Revenue-Generating Asset

If you're not ready to sell your home now, consider turning it into an asset that generates revenue or reduces expenses for the extended family. An easy and low risk way is to rent empty bedrooms on Airbnb or Home Away.

1. Set Up an Airbnb or Home Away Rental

I recently stayed in the lovely home of Diane and Wayne Keyes, a couple in their late 50s who have invited guests into their gorgeous Victorian home in the Orlando area. Built in 1890, this historic home was beautifully restored and updated to provide the perfect place to raise their family. Recent empty nesters in their mid-50s, they rattled around in their lovely 3,600 square foot home after the kids were grown, but loved it and didn't want to sell.

They accidently eased into renting rooms by first hosting European exchange students, and later by providing free housing to several members of a college baseball team, who were staying in the area for a multi-week summer training program. They enjoyed visiting with young people in the evenings and on weekends so much, that about two years ago they started renting rooms on Airbnb. They have loved it ever since.

They maintain their private bedroom and bath on the ground floor, and share common rooms including a fully-remodeled kitchen, spacious TV room, large library and billiards salon, formal living room, laundry facility, and inside and outside porches. Upstairs are three bedrooms and a shared bath, which they rent together for a family or group, avoiding having strangers share the single upstairs bathroom. Visitors can enjoy the lovely outdoor pool and hot tub, and the spacious grounds.

They charge very modest rent and have at least one room rented pretty much all the time. The rental income pays for utilities and maintenance and lets them enjoy their lovely home without torturing themselves with the question, "*Should we downsize and save money? Perhaps this is an option for your lovely home.*"

2. Care For Children In Your Home

Another option is to turn part of your home into a daycare. The average cost of daycare in the US is $611 per month per child but can vary by market between $250 to $1,200 monthly, according to *www.HowMuchIsIt.com*.

One friend has four grandbabies under the age of five. She opted to retire from her job as a private school aide to care for all four grandbabies in her home. By running a grandma daycare, both her daughter and daughter-in-law can take full time teaching jobs, earning good salaries, and put the combined $3,000 they save each month into bank accounts for down payment on future homes. Since she is caring for family members, she doesn't need a daycare license. Plus she is able to spend quality time with her grandchildren during the day, visit with her kids when they drop off and pick up the kids each morning and afternoon, and then relax with her husband when he gets home from work.

Another option is to operate a licensed daycare in your home, possibly taking care of your grandchildren as well as other children. You must follow state and city guidelines, perhaps become licensed, and submit to inspections, but at such high costs for daycare, it can be a profitable option.

Don't want to work so hard? Operate a daycare at night or over the weekend. Many American parents work on a shift basis, and employees in the medical, tourism, military, and hospitality sectors have a difficult time finding off-hours day care or babysitting services. Take the money you earn and put it towards your retirement nest egg while you enjoy your lovely home when the kiddies have gone home.

3. Convert Your Home Into a Private Care Home

There is a crisis in eldercare in America, with nursing home care costing between $4,000 and $7,000 per month or more for private-pay facilities. Social Security and perhaps Veterans Death Benefits may contribute a couple thousands per month, but that still leaves a huge gap, which will eat up a life savings in no time at all, leaving nothing for heirs or a surviving spouse.

When that happens, Medicaid may kick in and pay a pittance, leaving the infirm elderly in shoddy nursing homes with dozens of people sitting in wheelchairs sleeping slumped over in a group TV room — you've seen them in television shows, movies and sadly, probably in real life as well.

Another much more attractive option is small private care homes, owned by individuals instead of huge institutional management groups. In addition to providing far superior care and one-on-one attention, they offer you a benefit — a very attractive cash flow of several thousand dollars a month. They can be for seniors, Alzheimer's patients, or otherwise disabled individuals, often supported by disability insurance or Medicaid.

Traditional residential real estate rentals are risky. If you decide to rent your existing three- or four-bedroom home as a traditional rental, you can earn $1,300 to $2,000 per month (depending on the market). After property taxes, mortgage, interest, insurance and maintenance, you can net $500 to $1,000 per month maximum. If your tenants trash the house, fail to maintain the yard, paint the bedrooms black, kick holes in the drywall, or smoke like chimneys, you could lose all that profit. If they abandon the house or remain in the property without paying rent, you'll have to sue to evict, which can take months and thousands of dollars.

Enter the joy of a private care home, which provides $10,000–$15,000 of monthly gross rent deposited like clockwork into your bank account by Uncle Sam. After all expenses, this investment can spin off $3,000–$5,000 a month in operating profits, even after paying for round-the-clock staffing.

Susan Blumhorst, founder of Senior Path Specialists, opened my eyes to this opportunity when I was looking for options to care for my 95-year old mom with Alzheimer's.

I visited a four-bedroom group home just three miles from where I live in a safe neighborhood. It was clean, quiet, and comfortable, and staffed by a live-in caregiver who tends to the needs of the four residents with tenderness and compassion. One resident had Parkinson's disease and another suffered from chronic emphysema. A third was in the final stages of Alzheimer's, and the caregivers had arranged a second bed in the largest bedroom so the patient's husband could spend the night with her after work.

The live-in caregiver prepares home-cooked meals for each resident that they like or can tolerate. The sunny patio can be accessed by wheelchair, and on cool days the patients like to sit outside in the sunshine. I left feeling relieved that we can care for my mom with dignity when we can no longer do so in our home, even with hospice care.

When Susan explained the economics of a private care home, I was impressed! The first step is to find an appropriate single-story four- or five-bedrooms home (which can include a library or bonus room that can be converted to a private bedroom.) You may own just such a home now!

In Texas, it should cost no more than $230,000 and often as little as $150,000 to buy. With another $15,000–$20,000 for modifications and equipment — wheelchair ramps, a roll-in shower, easy-to-clean and sanitize flooring, safety features on doors and patios, safety gates, a covered driveway and an easy-to-access garage with a wheelchair ramp to the home, etc. — you'll be set up for Uncle Sam's "clockwork" checks. As the owner of the home, you are responsible for mortgage and interest, property tax, insurance, maintenance, and utilities.

Susan and her team do the rest. They hire, train and manage the staff, enroll the patients, work with Medicare, Medicaid, Veterans Affairs, Hospice, private medical and disability insurance, and other organizations to pay for the monthly care of the patients, which should run around $3,500 to $5,000 per patient — around half of what a larger nursing home costs for much less personalized care. She works with the different governmental groups to increase benefits if needed to secure appropriate care.

Hospice or government-paid nurses, doctors and aides often visit to check on the patients. Susan says that a private care home in Texas with four or fewer patients isn't regulated by the state or county, although her properties would easily pass.

Susan's company earns a percentage of the rents collected, giving them a vested interest in managing an efficient, desirable, and profitable home. She says the investor partners who own the houses earn around $50,000–$60,000 per year, and see a profit by month three or four when the home is fully occupied. If you choose to actually work in the home, rather than keep it as a passive investment, you can earn even more.

Due to the amount of hands-on attention they provide, Susan and her team only work with homes in San Antonio. But a number of other companies around the country provide consulting or partnerships to set you up with your own private care home. Susan says that residential care homes are booming in California, Oregon and Washington, among other states. It takes knowing the ropes, understanding the local governmental regulations, having a steady supply of qualified staff for both live-in and fill-in attendants, and much more to be successful. So I encourage you to get reliable help before choosing to do this on your own.

A year ago I went to a real estate investing seminar. The very wealthy investor-instructor talked about these same economics, and heartily recommended this as a lucrative real estate investment. He owned six such homes, and they were so profitable that he could offer top-of-the-line services to the residents: mobile beauty salons, monthly manicures, pedicures, and massages, video-conferencing with family members, a mobile library, even a weekly dress up dinner with candles and a violinist! He often books singers or entertainers to run the circuit of all his properties. Needless to say, he had no vacancies and long waiting lists of patients waiting to get in!

If you have a home and are trying to downsize or want passive income, this is definitely an option worth exploring!

Downsizing Takes Time and Money

Selling a house can be a very time-consuming process. It can require hundreds of hours of sorting, de-cluttering, clearing out, packing up and getting ready to move. Then it takes even more time, effort and money to fix up your house to sell it for top dollar. This can delay a move for months and cost you tens of thousands of dollars.

I've personally had two horror stories with selling my homes. Years ago, I was living in a lovely large home with a guest house, pool and two acres of oak trees in Florida. I got a job offer to move to San Antonio, which was a good career decision and very attractive financially. But it took me more than four months to make needed repairs and upgrades to make the house "sellable" — replace the island cook top, fix wobbly railings on the back porch, completely rescreen the huge screen pool enclosure, update the guesthouse kitchen, and much more. I ended up flying back and forth between San Antonio and Florida to deal with home inspectors, repairmen, roofers, realtors, and others. I couldn't enroll my son in school until the old house sold and I could close on the new one, so I had to leave him in Florida during the transition. He ended up starting the school year there, then transferring a month into the academic year when I finally had a utility bill proving I was a school district resident. All of this was happening while I was trying to impress the boss at a new job!

More recently, I had another unbelievable real estate mess. San Antonio has been one of the best real estate markets in the US for several years, with houses selling on average in less than 30 days. The market was hot, so I decided to downsize from my big half-empty two-story home to a one-story house with tile floors to care for my elderly mother.

I spent the spring and summer of 2016 cleaning out decades of old papers and business records, furnishings from four different homes stored in the attic, storage shed and garage, closets full of clothing that no longer fit, old furniture, kids' toys, moldy camping gear, long-gone hobby supplies, and just too-much-stuff in general. Somehow I felt that it had too much value to throw away, even though it wasn't of any use. Sound familiar?

I moved into my new smaller one-story rental home, leaving behind everything that didn't fit — a whole houseful! I scheduled a professional estate sale three weeks later, but it rained during the key sales days, reducing my expected sales by more than half, and leaving me with a house still full of stuff. I held my own rain check "estate sale" the following weekend, which didn't make a dent in the amount of stuff but did in my time — a whole week! I had painters and carpet installers scheduled to come in the next week and the house was still full! I ended up donating it all. A crew of volunteers from a local charity packed up boxes and loaded as much as they could into a 26' moving truck, packed to the gills! There was *still* so much left over — all the unsellable junk that no one wanted. I ended up paying to have it hauled to the dump.

That was just the start. Today, home inspectors are ruthless, and buyers want every single thing they note fixed, whether it is significant or not. I had to replace the roof ($17,000), all carpet with wood laminate and new textured carpets ($6,000), repaint inside and out ($4,000), make lots of repairs to fascia and siding ($2,500) — the list was very long and very expensive. The house prep took much more time than anticipated.

Fortunately, I sold the house at top dollar the first week it was on the market. The day before closing, the deal fell through because the buyer's ex-wife caused legal problems. After losing a month, I had to put the house back on the market. We were four weeks into the school year, sales had slowed down, so the house, which did not show well when the leaves had fallen, sat empty for six months, doubling my housing expenses — painful.

Eight months later, I got another qualified buyer and wrote a contract at a price $20,000 below the first sale. The buyers had to move fast to release furnishings from military storage and enroll their three girls in summer school, so we included a rent-to-close clause in the contract, allowing them to move in two weeks before closing. I disposed of the furnishings left to stage the house. The day before closing, the buyers emailed the realtor stating that they were backing out. I couldn't believe my luck. When I drove by the next day, I saw that the house was indeed empty!

Needless to say, I got a new realtor, who advised me to drastically drop the price again. Following his advice, I dropped the price week by week to $37,000 below appraised and Zillow price! His promised marketing plan never materialized, and during the six-week peak summer sales period, only 13 people even visited the house.

I fired him fast, then hired yet another realtor, along with his wife, an interior decorator and real estate stager. Based on her advice, I replaced all the countertops with granite ($6,000), and all bathroom hardware, lighting fixtures, and door hardware with new brushed nickel fixtures (another $3,000). We rented beautiful staging furniture for the whole downstairs ($3,000), bought new stainless kitchen sink, faucets, oven and glass cook top ($1,500), and replaced kitchen lighting and all ceiling fans with brushed nickel finishes ($2,000).

We raised the price back to that of the second sale, and after sitting empty for 13 months, we finally closed at $17,000 below appraised value.

This housing fiasco cost me over $75,000 and a year of work and frustration — almost the full amount the home had appreciated in value over 14 years! I paid off overextended credit cards and put the remaining equity into investments instead of housing.

Imagine if I had been transferred to a different city and had to fly back and forth to handle all this mess, or tried to do all this when I was even older and not as healthy?

Everyone says this was just incredibly back luck, and a real fluke that two buyers abandoned their contracts. But part of me thinks it happened so I could share with you and others what can happen when we sell our home at a later stage in life.

The good news is I am very happy in my new cozier, easy to maintain rental home. When something goes wrong, I call the landlord and it is fixed. I have reduced my housing expense by more than half, and have substantially plumped up my retirement piggy bank. I have the flexibility to leave when I want, and funds available to rent my dream home on that white sandy beach. Overall, I feel lighter, happier and less stressed. And I am making positive headway towards transitioning to the lifestyle I crave. Perhaps you will choose to do the same.

23

LOWER EXPENSES TO YOUR RETIREMENT LEVEL NOW

I suggest you check out *www.madfientist.com*, to learn from Brandon how to retire first and then get rich. The author will walk you through the steps (and finances) to downsize and lighten up, so you can retire now, rather than maintaining a more expensive lifestyle that requires you to work decades longer.

He recommends that you calculate your current living expenses and budget in detail, and also what your budget will be for your desired retirement lifestyle, then figure out how much you will need to earn monthly to achieve it.

Just think — if you can eliminate expenses one-by-one to reach your retirement-level budget, which you fund through Social Security, passive investments or part-time gigs, you can retire now! Why work to pay for your house, when you can fund the lifestyle you want instead? You may choose to bring yourself closer to living where and how you want rather than being tied to a physical asset in a fixed location that absorbs the vast majority of your income.

I am following his plan, and it feels good!

Once you begin this journey, you will find many resources to provide valuable insights and guidance. I suggest starting with *The 4-Hour Workweek* by Tim Ferris and *The Millionaire Next Door* by Thomas J. Stanley. They provide valuable help with how to scale down, live more frugally, invest more wisely, convert liabilities into assets, generate passive income, and much more.

The flip side of the equation is to increase income, especially mobile or flexible earnings, to reach your goal faster. That's where the job comes in.

Regardless of whether you are fully employed, unemployed, or looking for less stress and more time, it's important to think now about how you want to live in a year, five years, ten years, and into the future.

A key question is will it be easier to make and execute hard choices when you are older and possibly in worse health? Or are you willing to bite the bullet and start the journey of personal and financial flexibility now, making some tough but life-changing choices.

24

NOW'S THE TIME TO REINVENT YOUR CAREER

We started our careers during the era of mandatory retirement after 30 years of work, with a pension, a gold watch and golf or bridge as the options for spending our "golden years." All that has now changed.

We've lived through dramatic shifts in how companies are run, how the workplace is structured, and how employers recruit and hire talent.

As we age, our career goals and opportunities may also be changing. We may be secure and happy in our career, or unable to find a job or get a promotion. Many of us are forced to work just for medical insurance, with options opening only when we reach the age of Medicare and Social Security which free us from a huge financial liability and provide a steady income stream.

The important thing is that we *do* have options to earn a living if we choose to do so.

If your goal is to keep or find a job in Corporate America, you now have the insights, tools and resources to leverage your experience and connections to overcome objections and increase your hireability.

Congratulations on filling your knowledge bank so you can forge ahead into the future boldly and confidently. After reading this book, you know how to:

- Improve your computer and technology skills;
- Access resources to help you embrace lifelong learning and earn credentials that enhance your marketability — often for free;
- Take bold, scary steps to look as youthful as possible;
- Communicate with younger recruiters, colleagues and bosses;
- Build and upgrade your personal brand through networking, social media, and the effective use of powerful job search tools such as LinkedIn;
- Rethink your lifestyle and goals to create a new vision of a fulfilling life and career as you age.

I wish you great success and joy as you explore a whole new world of options for investing your time, energy, intellect, and creativity as you age. To me, the "Golden Years" are all about creating the life we choose to live.

Go bravely into your future of meaningful existence and profitable work, how and where you choose to do it.

Bon Voyage!

TAKE THE NEXT STEP TO FIND MEANINGFUL EMPLOYMENT

While I was writing this book, I discovered dozens of interesting, attractive and profitable jobs available to just about anyone with the basic credentials and a willingness to work. I started writing about them as a section of this book, but it grew so long that it became a whole new book. It's called *101 Great Jobs You Can Find Today*, and it will soon become available on *Amazon.com*, *GoRead.com*, and on my website *www.BrandYouGuide.com*.

Most of the featured jobs pay more than $15 an hour, and many offer $20 an hour or more. Many provide great benefits and are respectable employment for any professional, even if we had never considered then when we were younger.

A whole section of the book is devoted to starting your own business to offer innovative services or products that are in demand. There's information on buying an existing business with a steady and predictable cash flow, investing in a franchise, or jumping into entrepreneurial ventures.

Another section covers finding high-paying professional gigs, which are contract positions, which are expected to represent almost half of all jobs in the next decade. Many of these jobs offer the choice of full time or flexible schedules and work-at-home positions.

101 Great Jobs You Can Find Today is a companion guide to this book, geared to helping you find jobs for mature professionals quickly and that require little or no additional skills or credentialing.

I believe in the power of storytelling, so I share life stories of people who have opted for these jobs, so you can "try them on for size" vicariously. I also detail the salary or earnings potential, education or training needed, and the pros and cons of the different positions, so you have a good idea if it's a potential fit.

This book will be released in early 2019. Signup at *www.ReinventMyCareerPlease.com* to be on the mailing list for news of the release date.

MEET THE AUTHOR

I'm Diane Huth, and I love helping other people achieve their goals by leveraging my expertise and decades of experience in branding and marketing.

I'm also a university professor of marketing, branding and career development at Texas A&M University and The University of the Incarnate Word, both in San Antonio.

I'm also known as the "Accidental Career Coach."

I've worked in marketing forever (more than 30 years — yikes!) and I have loved at least 95% of everything I've done. I've run marketing departments for large companies like Johnson & Johnson, Frito-Lay, Mission Foods, and Nestlé that took me all over the world. I was also a founder and part owner of entrepreneurial companies such as Skinny Snacks and Biovideo.

I've screened thousands of résumés, interviewed hundreds of job candidates, hired scores of employees, and have mentored at least thirty interns.

For more than ten years I've been a Senior Innovation Strategist for Prodigy Works, creating breakthrough new product and innovation programs for leading national brands and companies.

Recently, I started teaching marketing and branding to college students at two different universities in my spare time, and I was shocked to learn how unprepared they were for their upcoming job search. I wrote my first book *BRAND YOU! To Land Your Dream Job* to help them (and you) find and land your ideal position.

As a result of positive feedback to that book, and requests from baby boomer friends and colleagues struggling to find well-paid jobs, I wrote this book to help mature professionals keep, find or create meaningful, enjoyable and profitable employment as long as they wish to work.

While writing this book, two more books "happened." The first is *101 Great Jobs You Can Find Today*, which showcases a wide range of jobs you might not have thought of, but which might just be right for you today. They all pay a decent wage, require minimum training, and are relatively easy to land without a substantial investment of time or money.

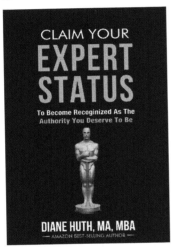

The second book is *Create Your Expert Status*, which walks you step-by-step through the advanced stages of personal branding, to leverage roles or positions to establish you as an acclaimed expert in your field, a recognized authority and celebrity in your own right. It's personal branding on steroids.

All my books can be purchased on *Amazon.com, GoRead.com*, and at my website *www.BrandYouGuide.com*.

I will launch the **Reinvent Your Career EXPO and Job Fair** on Saturday, January 26, 2019 in San Antonio to help you learn firsthand all these great insights and meet and speak with many of the recruiters and experts who can turn your dream into a reality. You will be able to attend remotely by livestreaming. Sign up online at *www.ReinventYourCareerEXPO.com*.

In 2019 we intend to bring the EXPO to dozens of other cities around the country, in conjunction with local workforce development organizations. If you would like more information about hosting or sponsoring the event, please contact me at *Diane@ReinventYourCareerEXPO.com*.

I am active every day on Facebook, Linkedin, Twitter, Instagram, YouTube and Pinterest, posting articles, memes, quotes, videos, tips and techniques, quizzes, contests and more to help you in your career development. You can also contact me directly at *Diane@BrandYouGuide.com*. I hope to hear from you!

THANKS TO VERY SPECIAL PEOPLE

Deep thanks go out to these wonderful friends and colleagues who helped to make this book come to life:

Carole Fawcett of Mindful Connections, professional editor and manuscript Sherpa — contact her at *www.amindfulconnection.com*

Christy Collins of Constellations Book Services, incredible interior designer of the book — find her at *www.constellationbookservices.com*

Venkata RamaRao.K — fabulous designer of the book cover. You can reach her by email at *cityzenpower@gmail.com*

Carla Schworer, fellow T-Bird alumni, FEMA specialist, and non-profit guru, of Las Vegas NV, for loving editing and encouragement

Miguel Castricciones, my right hand all around helper, graphic designer, video editor, and more, from Cainta, Philippines

Brook Carey of Schertz TX, career coach, founder of Executeam SW Business Consulting, and franchising guru

Lyndie O'Toole of Orange County CA, friend, mentor, research pro, and more

Steve Valdez, King of the Quinceañera, and author of *Quinceañera Planner* and *Debut of the Princess*, who is coordinating the book tour to launch this book

IMAGE LICENSES

Most images used in this book were licensed from *Dreamstime.com*, or are proprietary images created especially for this book. Logos of recommended companies, publications, and online resources or websites were sourced online from the respective sites. If you feel any images were used inappropriately or without permission, please contact me immediately at *Diane@BrandYou-Guide.com* so they can be removed.

REINVENT YOUR CAREER RESOURCE GUIDE

Tech UP! Technology Skills Improvement Programs

Grow With Google — https://grow.google — free training for businesses, organizations and individuals

EdX.org — Harvard University's professional tech degree program

Local community colleges — free and low-cost college programs

Adult education classes through school districts

YouTube Tech training video channels and websites— *TutorialWebsite.com, TutorialsPoint.com., W3Schools.com, ASP.net*

Udemy.com — 65,000+ online courses

Lynda.com — LinkedIn's membership site for training classes

LinkedIn Learning — *https://learning.linkedin.com/*

Coursera.com — online courses

MediaBistro.com — online courses

Kim Komando Show — *www.komando.com*

Meet Up — *www.meetup.com* — local activity-based groups

Apple Store — free technology classes to learn to use Apple products

Microsoft Store — Free tech classes at local retail stores

Tech magazines — *PC World, Technology Review, Popular Mechanics, Computer Power User, Science News*

KAlliance.com — unlimited classes for $199 annually

Ed2Go.com — work at your own speed online classes offered by colleges for credit

RightSkill.com — Online training offered by Career Builder and Capella Learning

Lifelong Learning Resources

Employer tuition reimbursement programs

www.Starbucks.com/careers/college-plan — Free tuition to ASU online for employees working 20+ hours weekly

Non-profit Job Training Services

US Department of Labor, state Departments of Labor

Goodwill Industries — www.Goodwill.org

AARP — www.AARP.org

Dress For Success — www.DressForSuccess.org

Resources For a More Youthful Appearance

Hair restoration, regrowth and transplantation — Hair Club for Men — www.hairclub.com, Bosley Hair Restoration — www.Bosley.com

Care Credit — www.CareCredit.com — low- or no-interest financing for medical services

Mary Kay Cosmetics — www.MaryKay.com

Careington Dental — www.CareingtonDental.com

Invisilign invisible braces — www.Invisalign.com

Smile Direct Club — www.SmileDirectClub.com — one-stop invisible teeth straightening

Clear Choice Dental — www.ClearChoice.com — one-stop dental implants

Sono Bello — Comprehensive body contouring, liposuction, and face lifts — www.Lipo.SonoBello.com

Lifestyle Diet Programs — Jenny Craig, Nutrisystem, South Beach Diet, Paleo Diet, Atkins Diet

Womens fashions — Chicos — www.Chicos.com, Jostar — www.JostarUSA.com

Men's Fashion Retailers — Burlington — *BurlingtonCoatFactory.com*, J C Penny — *www.JCPenny.com*, Saks Off 5th — *www.SakOff5th.com*, Macy's — *www.Macys.com*

Technology and Business Tools

GeekSquad Protection Program — *www.Geek-Squad-Tech-Support.com* — online remote computer tech support provided by Best Buy

Carbonite — *www.Carbonite.com* — Remote backup for computer files

Microsoft 360 Office Suite — basic business communication subscription program

GoDaddy — *www.GoDaddy.com* — one-stop website and domain services

Low-cost online logo design and branding options — Upwork — *www.Upwork.com*, 99 Designs — *www.99Designs.com*

VistaPrint — *www.VistaPrint.com* — turnkey design and printing of business cards

Online Portfolio sites — LinkedIn — *www.LinkedIn.com*, Pathbrite *www.Pathbrite.com*, Issuu — *www.Issuu.com*, Carbonmade — *www.CarbonMade.com*, DROPR *www.dropr.com*, Cargo Collective — *www.CargoCollective.com*, Behance — *www.Behance.com*, Coroflot — *www.Coroflot.com*

VenturePoint — *www.VenturePointSA.com* — coworking remote office hub

Frugal at Fifty Lifestyle Options

Home repurposing options — Airbnb — *www.airbnb.com*, Home Away — *www.HomeAway.com*

Senior Path Specialists — experts in establishing private care homes — *www.SeniorPathSpecialists.com*

The 4-Hour Workweek, by Tim Ferris

The Millionaire Next Door, by Thomas J. Stanley

Rich Dad Poor Dad by Robert Kiyosaki

Lifehacker.com — Blog for low-cost living

INDEX

101 Great Jobs You Can Find Today
   144, 177
99 Designs 185

A

AARP 11, 12, 13, 47, 127
   2013 Study 11
   2017 Study 13
   Job Training 47, 157
ACA Act Of 1976 10
Accessories 66, 68, 71
ADEPT 46
Adaptable Equipment Proficiency
   Testing 46
Adopt Younger Actions 37, 74-79
Adult Education Programs 41
Age Discrimination in Employment
   Act (ADEA) 15
Ageism 11, 17
Agile Employment 22, 162
Airbnb 40, 165, 166
   Data University 40
Alumni Association 93, 94
   Networking 87, 89, 90, 91, 93, 94,
     95, 105, 111, 123, 131, 175
American Marketing Association
   47, 91
   PCM Certification 47
Apple Store 43
ASP.Net 42
Atkins Low-Carb Diet 63
Attaché Case 71, 72

B

Become Flexible 162
Behance.Net 135
Behiring.Com 114
Biovideo 6
Blepharoplasty 61
   Lower Eye Lid Surgery 61
   Upper Eye Lid Surgery 61
Body Contouring 64
Bosley Hair Restoration 53
BRAND YOU! To Create Your Expert
   Status 180
BRAND YOU! To Land Your Dream
   Job 87, 114, 131
Brook Carey 181
   Unemployment Study 2, 11, 12, 13
Burlington 71

C

Capella Learning 48
Carbonite 76
Carbonmade 135
Care Credit 56, 60, 61, 65
Career Builder 48, 91
Careington Dental Plan 59
Cargo Collective 135
Carla Schworer 181
Carole Fawcett 181
Cataract Surgery 56, 61, 79, 154
Chicos Fashions 68
Citizenship And Work Status 123
Clearchoice Dental Implant Centers
   59

Community Colleges Career
   Training 41
Commuting Costs 140
Company Email Address 100, 115
Competency-Based Degrees 49
Computer Power User 43
Coroflot 135
Cousera 47
Curriculum Vitae 127
Cursive 21, 83

D
Diane Huth 179
Downsizing 30, 31, 96, 170
Dr. Chrissann Merriman 49
Dreamstime.com 182
Dress for Success 47, 66, 127
   Job Training 47, 157
Dropbox 83
DROPR 135

E
Earnings Expectations 139
Ed2Go 48
Edx.Org 40
Elevator Pitch 131, 133
Eliminate Debt 162
ERISA 15,

F
Facebook 16, 17, 57, 60, 74, 75, 94,
   104, 109
   Managing Your Profile 109-110
Facelift 62, 67,
Family Child Care
Fashion Makeovers For Men 69
   Shirts 69, 70, 71
   Shoes 71

Socks 71
Suits 69, 71
Federal Reserve Bank of San
   Francisco Study 11
Fitness 6, 48, 64, 68, 77, 149
Fiverr 101
Flexible Workplace 23
Frugal At Fifty 161, 163

G
Geek Squad Protection Program 75
George Hempe 48, 89
Glasses 55, 56, 60, 61, 72, 79, 143,
   154
Gmail Account 83
GoMobile 74
GoDaddy 100, 101
Godaddy Website Builder 101
Goodwill Industries 47
Google 16, 25, 40, 74, 76, 83, 93,
   112, 113, 122, 127
Grow With Google 40
Google+ 112, 113

H
Hair Club For Men 53
Hair Color, Cut, Style 52, 53, 72
Hard Copy Portfolio 130, 133,
   134,
Heavy Equipment Colleges of
   America 46
Heidi Shierholz 12
Home Away Rental 166
Home Office Deductions 98, 140,
   141
Hootsuite 113
Hospitality Committee 91, 92

I

If You Win the Lottery Today 152,
153,155, 157
Image Licenses 182
Invisilign Braces 60
Issuu 135

J

J C Penny 71
Jenny Craig 63
Jeunesse® Instantly Ageless™ Wrinkle
Cream 60
Job Search Tools 129, 131, 133,
175
Job Service Agency 41
Job Services Organization 47, 48
Free Skills Training 47, 48
Jostar Microfiber Fashions 68

K

Kallince.Com 48
Key Volunteer Committees 91
Kim Komando 42

L

Laptop Computers 23, 24, 75, 76, 77
Laser Teeth Whitening 57
Legal Zoom 97
Letters Of Recommendation 29, 30,
129, 130
Licensed Daycare 167
Lifestyle Changes 149, 151
Linkedin 31, 83, 87, 93, 95, 101,
105, 106, 107, 108, 109, 111, 113,
115, 117, 122, 135, 176
Linkedin Career Plan 105
Linkedin Learning 45, 47

Liposuction 64
Luis Escobar 24
Lynda 42
Lyndie O'Toole 181

M

Mac Computers 33, 76
Macy's 71
Madfientist.com 173
Makeup 24, 56, 57, 61, 66, 72
Manicures 65, 170
Mary Kay Cosmetics 57
Maslow Hierarchy of Needs 156
MediaBistro 47
Medical Insurance Costs 1, 10, 13,
19, 78, 137, 141, 144, 175
Meet Up Groups 43
Membership Committee 92
Microsoft 360 Office Suite 83
Microsoft Store 43
Miguel Castricciones 181
Military Service 123
Minimize Physical Limitations 78

N

NCOO 46
National Crane Certification
Organization 46
Networking 87, 89, 90, 91, 93, 94,
95, 97, 99, 101, 105, 111, 123,
131, 175
Conduct Interviews 94
Events 90
Non-Verbal Messaging 79
Nursing Home Costs 169
Nutrisystem 63

O

Online Portfolio 72, 105, 115, 134, 135,

Own Consulting Company 87, 97, 101, 103, 122,

P

Pathbrite 135

PC World 43

Pedicure 65, 170

Personal Trainer 64

Pinterest 104, 112

Plexiderm 61

Politics 84, 126

Poor Man's Docking Station 77

Popular Mechanics 43

Pre-Pay Expenses 161

Presentations 28, 39, 82, 105, 109

Private Care Home 167, 168, 169

Prodigy Works 6

Professional Associations 47, 90, 110, 122, 134

    Networking 90

Professional Passion Matrix 145

Propublica 16

Public Relations Committee 93

R

References 71, 84, 129, 130, 134

Reinvent Your Career EXPO 216

Résumé 29, 30, 66, 71, 87, 93, 97, 100, 103, 105, 106, 114, 115, 116, 117, 118, 119, 120, 121, 122, 124, 125, 126, 127, 128 , 130, 134, 135

    Career Objective 116, 117

    Education 106, 114, 119, 122

    Formatting 115, 124, 127

    Grammar and Spelling 29, 128

    Name And Contact Information 115

    Online Submission 125

    Overview 109, 118, 125

    Personalization 126

    Photo 126

    Professional Experience 119, 120, 121

    Skills And Expertise 122

    Summary Of Skills 118

    Taboo Topics 126

    Title For Online Submission 124, 125

Retirement 1, 3, 4, 9, 10, 13, 14, 15, 137, 143, 144, 150, 161, 167, 172, 173, 175

Change In Concept 143, 144

Rightskill.com 48

S

Sabbatical 5, 95

Saks Off 5th 71

Salon.Com 16

SAS Shoes 67

Saving More 161

Science News 43

Scrum Teamwork Models 22

Share A Home 164

Slack App 21, 74, 82

Slideshare 109, 135

Smile Direct Club 60

Social Media 16, 43, 87, 94, 95, 101, 104, 105, 106, 107, 108, 109, 110, 111, 112, 113, 121, 122, 125, 132, 175

Social Security 1, 7, 9, 10, 13, 14, 34, 78, 98, 139, 144, 150, 157, 162, 167, 173, 175

    Average Monthly Benefits 10

Benefit Calculations 10
    Eligibility Age 9
Sono Bello 62
Starbucks 79
    College Degree Plan 45
    Morning Coffee 79
Start Ups 24, 31, 99
Symphony Multi-Focal Lenses 56

T
Taboo Topics 126
Technology Review 43
The 4-Hour Workweek 173
The American Crane School 46
The Baby Boomer Employment
    Crisis 12
The Intern Movie 25
The Internship Movie 25
The Millionaire Next Door 173
The Paleo Diet 63
The South Beach Diet 63
The Unemployable Generation 1
Toastmasters 146
Tuition Reimbursement Programs
    45
Tutorialspoint.Com 42
Tutorialwebsite.Com 42
Twitter 81, 104, 111,112, 113
    Follow Journalists on Twitter 111

U
Udemy 42, 48
Upwork 101
USAA 22

V
Venturepoint 24

Vista Print 102
Volunteer 32, 41, 90, 91, 92, 94, 100,
    110, 122, 123, 126, 129, 134, 148,
    151, 155, 157, 171,

W
W3Schools.com 42
Walk Briskly 77
Wardrobe Makeover 65, 66,
Wearable Technology 75
Weight Watchers 63
Why Companies Hire Millennials
    18-25
Why Companies Should Hire Baby
    Boomers 25-35
Willingness To Relocate or Travel
    123
Wired 43
Workforce Solutions Alamo 48, 89
Write Short And Cryptically
Www.Brandyouguide.Com
    32, 149

Y
Younger Boss 84, 159
Your Own Company 97-103
    Benefits 97, 98
    Branding 101, 103
    Business Card 101-103
    Domain Name 99-100
    Email Address 100
    Legal Structure 97
    Website 100
YouTube 112
    Training Videos 42

MORE BOOKS IN THE BRAND YOU! SERIES OF CAREER GUIDES

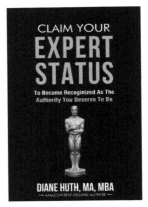

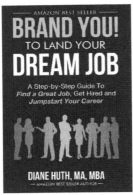

BEFORE YOU GO

If you enjoyed this book and found it to be valuable, please take just one more minute to write a brief review for Amazon, and hopefully give it a five-star rating.

It will give me feedback and help others in their journey to land their dream job as well. It really does matter to me, so thank you in advance!

Please go to https://goo.gl/mPfxMQ now to write your review.

Made in the USA
Middletown, DE
04 April 2019